HOPE

Our Longing for Home

D1249116

HOPE

Our Longing for Home

JOHN INDERMARK

UPPER
ROOM BOOKS®
NASHVILLE

HOPE: OUR LONGING FOR HOME
Copyright © 2007 by John Indermark
All rights reserved.

Cover design: GoreStudio Inc.
Cover photo: © AVTG/iStock
First printing: 2007

LIBRARY OF CONGRESS CATALOGING-IN-PUBLICATION DATA
Indermark, John, 1950–
    Hope: our longing for home / by John Indermark.
        p. cm.
    ISBN 978-0-8358-9921-5
    1. Hope—Biblical teaching. 2. Hope—Religious aspects—Christianity.
    I. Title.
    BS680.H7I53 2007
    234'.25—dc22   200730008

Printed in the United States of America

You have made us for yourself,
and our hearts are restless until they rest in you.

—SAINT AUGUSTINE

CONTENTS

ACKNOWLEDGMENTS

Writing a book on hope might seem a rather presumptive activity. As I have told more than one friend or colleague, writing on this theme is as much a searching for reason to live with hope in these days as it is an offering of what (and where) I have found cause to hope.

I begin by thanking Cathie Talbot, an editor with *Seasons of the Spirit* with whom I have worked and whom I am privileged to count as friend. Several years ago Cathie and her husband opened their home on Vancouver Island to my wife and me. The conversation after dinner turned to this book project on hope. Cathie suggested it would be interesting to bring in the thoughts and voices of others about hope's perceptions and questions in their lives. Subsequently, I contacted a number of colleagues and friends with a series of questions to elicit their ideas. Out of those responses came many of the quotes scattered through these pages. To them I offer thanks and gratitude:

- Jan Epton Seale: writer and teacher; McAllen, Texas
- Sharon Harding: curricula writer; Athabasca, Alberta
- Roddy Hamilton: writer and pastor in the Church of Scotland (and the only friend I have who has dined with the Queen of England); Clydebank, Scotland
- Lynn Longfield: General Presbyter of Olympia Presbytery; Tacoma, Washington
- Rebecca Grothe: editor for *Seasons of the Spirit* and *The Clergy Journal*; Hillsboro, North Dakota
- Carol Wehrheim, writer, editor, and teacher; Princeton, New Jersey
- Mark Miller, Transitional Interim Conference Minister, Pacific Northwest United Church of Christ; Seattle, Washington

I have also used several quotes from the writings of Jürgen Moltmann. His books *Theology of Hope* and *The Coming of God* provided valuable background reading as I prepared to write this. Those who want to delve seriously into the meaning of hope from the perspective of Christian faith would do well to immerse themselves in these works.

My relationship with Upper Room Books enters its tenth year as I submit this, and I continue to be the recipient of their good care in the process of moving from rough drafts to bound books. JoAnn Miller and now Lynne Deming have faithfully worked with me during the acquisition and submission stage. Rita Collett, as usual, has done her excellent work in the editing process.

The completion of the first draft came at an interesting juncture in my life. With the final chapter to go, I found myself undergoing surgery and then hospitalization for a week. When an infection set in midway through the hospital stay, words about hope took on a new urgency—as did the importance of hope's embodiment and expression through community. Human touch took on fresh meaning. Human compassion, or the lack thereof, from my caregivers became a quality experienced in a new light. To my wife and son, who sat beside me through that week and held on to me, often literally, I am grateful in a way that defies words—but still requires words.

Hope is that way too. You may well find that the words of this book fail to do full justice to the meaning and power of hope as you have experienced hope or as you earnestly seek its signs in an often unhopeful world. But even when hope escapes "capture" in words, hope still requires words as witness. Words that remind us of God's presence and ultimate purposes. Words that remind us that such presence and purposes can be conveyed in the most human of ways, in the company of others who love and care and who will see things through with us.

Prologue

HOPE

BEGINNING THE JOURNEY

Hebrews 11:8-16

---

*There is nothing very concrete about [hope],
and its use is very wishy-washy.*

REV. RODDY HAMILTON

Rev. Hamilton's words might seem an unusual opening to a book on hope. They do not reflect my core beliefs about hope. But I read his words and nod in sad agreement, because their implicit critique of what passes for hope is absolutely on target.

Too much that passes for hope among us is little more than wishful thinking disconnected from action taken in response. Too much that passes for hope reflects self-centered daydreaming about what would be nice for me and mine to the exclusion of any concrete consideration for you and yours. Too much that passes for hope wants to let go and let God, even in those matters where our gracious God waits and waits for us to act. To term such hope *wishy-washy* is gentle understatement. Such a parody of hope leaves us spiritually homeless, stripped of the calling and direction so vital in biblical faith.

Such false optimisms lead us nowhere of value. They are no better, and perhaps even more deceitful, than wearying pessimisms that abandon us in despair and cynicism. Sometimes we are seduced into thinking those are the only available options. Yet the writings of Israel and of the early church bear witness to a third option: the way of hope. The deep hopes of those communities resonate in the imagery of faith as a journey toward home. As the author of Hebrews puts it: "People who speak in this way make it clear that they are seeking a homeland." Hope involves finding where and to whom we and all creation belong and then having the trust and courage to start living in that direction.

Hope involves action, and action involves choices. Recall the story of Abraham. Hope in the form of trust in God's promises led to more than a warm, tingly feeling inside. Hope led to one foot placed in front of the other, again and again, until the old home city of Haran disappeared from sight and the new city . . . well, that's why it's hope. The new city never did clearly come into sight. But choices and actions did not wait until all was obvious. Abraham and Sarah walked. They chose to walk for the rest of their lives.

Sojourners is a favored biblical expression for such folks whose journey toward God's future transforms present attitudes and actions. This book invites us to be sojourners for the sake of God's future that serves as home for us and for all of creation. We walk and work, we choose and hope—*now*. In this moment, in this place. While hope keeps its eyes fixed on the future, hope also keeps feet planted firmly on the ground and hands thick in the mix of life lived now. Why? Because the journey begins here.

And the journey begins in community. In terms of this book *community* takes shape in several ways. Now and again you will read words from my colleagues on various aspects of hope. You have already heard from Roddy Hamilton. In the daily exercises you will from time to time be asked to reflect and act on portions of the readings that will lead you into the presence of others. For those of you who read this as part of a study group, community will take shape among those with whom you meet.

Finally, community plays a fundamental role in the way I have structured this work. Each chapter is joined to a particular biblical text. The scripture selections do not exhaust everything the Bible says on hope. Rather, the choices have to do with illuminating critical insights into hope's holding and embodying in life. You may even have noticed that the passages chosen fall in canonical order. That is, they follow the order in which their originating books appear in the

Bible. This ordering is not to imply some superimposed theory of progression, as if hope in Genesis were more "primitive" and in Revelation more "full." Rather, the ordering is to explore hope's weave throughout the whole biblical narrative so that we may better discern our place in hope's wider community.

Using This Book

This book contains three main sections: nine chapters, an appendix of spiritual exercises (one set per chapter), and a leader's guide for use in small-group study.

As noted above, each chapter keys on a biblical passage. Before you read the chapter, please read the passage that sets the stage for that chapter's issues, stories, and imagery of hope. I recommend that you read the chapter and then do the designated spiritual exercises. I strongly encourage you to follow this weekly regimen.

Day One: read the chapter.

Day Two: engage the first spiritual exercise designated for that chapter.

Day Three: engage the second spiritual exercise designated for that chapter.

Day Four: engage the third spiritual exercise designated for that chapter.

Day Five: engage the fourth spiritual exercise designated for that chapter.

Day Six: engage the fifth spiritual exercise designated for that chapter.

Day Seven: sabbath rest (meeting day if you are part of a group using this book).

If time permits, you might read through the entire book and then go back and reread one chapter at a time and engage the accompanying spiritual exercises.

The leader's guide outlines suggestions for a nine-session, small-group study of this resource. *Your work on the spiritual exercises will provide the foundation for the sessions* (see below). Even if you are not part of a small-group study, you might find some of the ideas in the guide helpful in exploring more deeply the readings and your practice of hope.

Using This Book for Lent / Easter

This book lends itself well to individual reading or to exploration in a group study that begins in Lent and extends into the first weeks of Easter. Such a schedule encourages a more intentional connection between the themes of Lent with the consequences of Easter. Use *Hope: Our Longing for Home* during this season as follows:

An individual would begin reading the book on the Monday of the week that includes Ash Wednesday. Using this schedule, you will be reading chapter 7 (on resurrection) during the week prior to Easter.

For group study, hold your session either the Sunday following Ash Wednesday or during the week after that Sunday. If you add an introductory session as described on page 141, move this schedule up a week. Following this schedule, those who meet on Sundays would explore chapter 7 on Easter Sunday (or the Sunday following, if you choose not to meet on Easter). Those who meet during the week would explore chapter 7 the week following Easter.

In all cases, this approach leaves two more weeks (chapters) of reading and exploring together during the season of Easter. Those concluding two chapters deal directly with issues raised by Easter faith and hope as we live in the "interim" between Jesus' raising and the coming of God's realm.

A Word on the Spiritual Exercises

The purpose of this book is *not* to give you information about hope, although it may do that. More importantly, it invites you to be *formed* by hope. The outcome sought is a life not simply more familiar with hope's meaning but one that practices hope in word and deed. How do you make the transition from words on a page to words embodied in conduct?

The spiritual exercises will offer a regular process for deepening your engagement with the texts of scripture and the chapters that flow from them. That process is by no means an invention of this author. Rather, it grows out of a tradition of "spiritual reading" (*lectio divina*) that has been used by Roman Catholics and Protestants for centuries. Each chapter will employ the same pattern, offering a sense of rhythm and continuity among them. The original pattern of *lectio divina* consisted of four elements: reading, meditation, prayer, and contemplation. More recently, some practitioners of this particular approach have added a fifth element: action. The spiritual exercises in this book will be grounded in those five movements.

Each week the first exercise will involve a practice of focused reading of the scripture text at hand. The second exercise will invite meditation on words and images from that text as well as reading the chapter. The third exercise will move into prayer in the opening of ourselves to holy presence. The fourth exercise will evoke some action related to practicing that aspect of hope. The fifth exercise will invite contemplation, a sabbath time of quiet and rest with these words and with this hope.

Begin the Journey

Welcome to these pages. Take time in their reading. Be open to the Spirit's leading. Wrestle with the questions that may arise. Walk with the vision that may come. And with our mothers and fathers in faith and for the sake of our children in faith, seek the homeland that brings God's promised future to bear on this journey we make now.

Chapter 1

HOPE

GROUNDING IN GRACE

Genesis 8:21-22; 9:8-17

Love for Christ and hope for him embrace
love and hope for the earth.
—Jürgen Moltmann

The year after my wife, Judy, and I bought our first and current home, we built a small arbor. It was one of those projects that moved quickly from desire ("wouldn't it be nice to have an arbor for the wisteria and honeysuckle") to purchase of materials ("let's not spend too much") to construction ("how quickly do you think we can get this done?"). Please hear the term *construction* very loosely. We used no piers or blocks to anchor the framework formed entirely of two-by-twos. We just dug four holes, stuck the footings in, and voilà! The first year all went well. Spindly vines and thin branches wrapped lightly through the arbor. Winter southwesters that year breezed through the structure. We did notice that during the heavier rains the footings flexed a bit. The next year we drove rods of rebar into the ground beside the four wooden footings and wired each footing to one of the rods. The following year we attempted to hold up the now sagging arbor by fastening it to one of the corner posts of the porch with a cable. The next year we returned home from a winter trip to find the arbor balancing precariously at a forty-five-degree angle against the picnic table, its footings pulled from the ground by the weight of the plants and the force of the wind.

Secure grounding would have been a good place to start on the original work of that arbor. It is a good place to start on this book about hope. Whether the project at hand involves lumber, words, or lives, groundwork needs to be done in order to set a foundation that will endure. This chapter aims to ground the meaning and practice of hope in a secure foundation. The foundation to which the biblical witness anchors hope is grace: God's favor for and seeking the good of not just humankind but the whole earth. The Bible's first formal account of covenant reveals such grace and grounding.

Noah

The Lord told Noah to build him an arky, arky,
The Lord told Noah to build him an arky, arky,
Build it out of gopher barky, barky, children of the Lord.

(from the children's song "Rise and Shine")

For some people the story of Noah remains on the level of lively choruses and preschoolers' introductions to Bible stories. It does, after all, have lots of animals and a pretty rainbow at the end. How toddlers comprehend what happened to all those who *didn't* go twosies by twosies into the ark, including Noah's not-so-friendly neighbors, means either suppressing parts of the narrative or impressing the image of a rather vengeful God on formative young spirits.

For others the story of Noah has taken on the trappings of an Indiana Jones saga. Rumors periodically fly and books occasionally publish tales about wooden relics on remote mountains in the Middle East sought by intrepid adventurers in the face of discouraging local authorities. The subtext of these searches seems to be that fragments of ancient cedar will lay to rest questions about biblical authority in general and the story of Noah in particular.

But what does the story of Noah have to do with hope and grace? In a word, the answer resides in *covenant*. For when the waters have settled, and Noah and his family and the animal duos step out on dry land to test legs too long at sea, God perceives something. Even with this radical act of housecleaning that has come at such a high cost of life, even with all of the change that a flood can wreak on landscape and human spirit, one thing has not been altered. One thing remains unchanged before the flood and after: Noah, which is to say, us. The movement and change has been on God's part. Verse 21 asserts God's view that "the inclination of the human heart is evil from youth." That is an almost verbatim assessment of the human condition made by God in Genesis 6:5. Then, God's response to that truth came in floodwaters covering the earth and its creatures. Now, God's response to that truth comes in a covenant enfolding the earth and its creatures.

That is a hard pivot to make on flannelgraph depictions of smiling elephants and rainbows breaking out of the clouds. It is hard to show a *before* and *after* picture of God to toddlers, much less adults, and explain the difference in a meaningful way. It is equally hard to prove any change of direction in divine intent toward humanity and creation by claiming alleged relics of a millennia-old seacraft. Such things, while both interesting and captivating, miss the heart of the story, a heart grounded in the trust that God has determined to go about things differently, given the constancy of our condition. Destruction, whether deserved or not, is rejected. Covenantal relationship midwifed by grace is the choice. Back in Genesis 6 God's assessment of the human condition is said to have grieved God's heart. It will not be the last time that those formed in the divine image will break God's heart. But that gets ahead of our story, a story concerned now with God's determination to move forward with these habits of the human heart by taking the path of grace.

God's covenant reveals how broad and decisive the path of grace will be. This text's unmistakable insistence that covenant is solely the act of God serves as yet another reminder that the grounding of our hope is in grace. Nothing Noah does or can do will evoke this relationship. God does not bargain. To the consternation of the democratically inclined, Noah does not participate in covenant's forming, conditions, or extent. All that falls to Noah is covenant's acceptance, and in some ways even that is beside the point. What God does in this situation is what God does. Sheer grace. Sheer gift.

To some of the dutiful among us, myself included, this may sound off-putting. *So if covenant is struck regardless of any movement or decision on my part, where is the hope in that?* Consider this. A child is born to parents. Nothing this child has done merits love. Love is freely and graciously given. As that child grows, even when mistakes are made and guidance is not followed and tantrums are thrown, that relationship—that *environment* of love—remains in place. Its expression by the parents may change according to circumstances. But in healthy family relationships the primal foundation of unconditional love continues. The child's lack of choice in that environment's creation and expression does not lessen its value. In some ways that environment's independence from "earning" or "deserving" on the part of the child ensures that it continues through difficult and even rebellious times.

The covenant with Noah establishes the *environment* of grace in which God holds us. The fact that we had no say in its decision or construction is its very protection. Since it is not ours ("ours" as in human) to decide, our decisions cannot make it pass out of existence. Since it is not ours to construct, neither is it ours to de-struct. This latter point is of extraordinary importance in connecting grace with our hope's grounding. No one, no power has the authority to negate this covenant. Only God can, and God has stamped this decision to covenant rather than destroy with the words *never again.* This gracious relationship known as covenant is the environment in which we live and move and have our being.

God will make other covenants with Abraham, Moses, and Jesus. But nowhere will you find in those covenants an abrogation of this first one with Noah. God does not replace one covenant with another. Build upon, yes. Focus, yes. But replace? No! As a result, at the foundation of every relationship with God we find this deep grounding in grace. What makes this grounding a channel of hope? First, consider the remarkable if not scandalous announcement of who and what God covenants with. Second, God makes two definitive promises that estab-

lish the nature of hope at the core of this relationship. To those characters and toward those promises we now turn our attention.

With You ... I Will ...

Somewhere in boxes of childhood memorabilia in our attic crawl
space are several scorecards from St. Louis Cardinal baseball games. I
remember nothing of those particular games. But looking at the
names of the starting lineup in the box score section and the listing of
the team roster summons my memory. Bob Gibson. Dal Maxvill. Mike
Shannon. For me, the names are larger than individual monikers. The
names call to mind particular teams: later than the days of Vinegar
Bend Mizell and Stan Musial, earlier than those of Ozzie Smith and
Willie McGee. They sound out associations with seasons great and
not so great. Their names specify those times and serve as my connections with those memories.

When God establishes covenant in Genesis 9, names specify this
relationship and serve as our connections to its partnering. To deem
this covenant with the name of Noah is a kind of theological shorthand. But lest shorthand become shortsighted, we need to remember
that Noah's name is not the only one invoked by God as partner to
this covenant. Every one—and every thing—named in Genesis 9
speaks to the breadth of that covenant's gracious grounding.

Noah heads the list: the obedient builder in the face of ridicule,
the dutiful herder of every animal clean and unclean, the original fash-
ioner of an altar. But Noah does not end the list. The circle grows
wider with the inclusion of Noah's "descendants." Covenant then and
now is about community. It is about the people of God standing
together on holy ground, in holy relationship. The ark is an early
symbol that God's acts of deliverance inevitably attempt to create a
new community. The term *descendants* offers another insight into the
nature of this covenant. It stretches across time. God covenants not
just with Noah's immediate family in his generation, God names as
partners all the children and cousins and far-flung ones yet to be born.

Covenant spans lifetimes and envelops future generations. All of human community—for the story states we are *all* descendants of Noah—finds invitation to ground its hopes on that foundation.

Yet even here, with the naming and inclusion of the entire human community, we have not exhausted the list of God's covenant partners. The names continue "with every living creature that is with you, . . . every living creature of all flesh that is on the earth." The environment of grace in which we are blessed to reside is not a human milieu alone. God's grace, God's covenant, extends here to the animals. Genesis 9:8-17 asserts no fewer than five separate times that God's covenant includes nonhuman life.

What a remarkable, baffling, and challenging assertion that speaks of covenant's wondrous inclusion of all life on earth. Baffling in that we do not know how to translate categories of covenant beyond human purposes. Challenging in that humanity has callously treated nonhuman life, not to mention our treatment of other human beings. God covenants here with all flesh, human and otherwise.

As if this were not enough, let us lift up the final name and partner identified with this covenant. When God speaks of the rainbow that will serve as covenant's sign, the author of Genesis frames God's words concerning the final partner in this way: "and it [the bow] shall be a sign of the covenant between me and the *earth*" (v. 13, italics added). Not only Noah, not only Noah's descendants, not only every living creature: God now declares the earth itself as included in this relationship. The Hebrew word used there is *'erets*, the common name for earth or land. This same word has been used throughout the Genesis 1 account of creation and the Genesis 6 account of the flood. The earth that had been God's creation, the earth that had been filled with violence, the earth that had been swept over by the waters and then dried by the wind that God made to pass over it: with this earth God now makes covenant.

For the stretch of the imagination it may take to conceive of what it means for God to covenant with animals, multiply that now with the inclusion of the earth in covenant. Earth-First! activists did not invent these words, nor are they edicts recently issued from the head-quarters of People for the Ethical Treatment of Animals. God reveals and seals these ancient words of covenant to and with Noah. Human-kind does not possess sole rights to covenant with God. These words signify God's covenanting with us and with all creation.

Earlier I wrote of the covenant with Noah as an environment of grace in which we and all creation live. The inclusion of animals and earth in this covenant by God's declaration brings fresh meaning and urgency to the term *environment*. If we take seriously the nature of this covenant, the environment of grace embraces the whole of our natural environment. People of faith will disagree on the specific practices of human activity that fall within the bounds of faithful stewardship of land and creation. But the covenant with Noah severely questions any attitude that treats the earth and its creatures in purely utilitarian ways—that is, their only value derives from their value to us. God's naming the land and its creatures as covenant partners reminds us of their unique value and place in and of themselves. The extinction of species, destruction of land, and disregard for future generations are not mere by-products of human progress. They are breaches of covenant. Covenant calls us to responsible living by reminding us that God's environment of grace enfolds all of our natural environment, even as it bestows its promises upon all its partners.

Standing on the Promises

Promises. At times they may be cajoled or bullied from another, extracted only under duress or threat. At other times they float free in our direction, unsummoned, their origins as mystifying to us as they are necessary for our well-being. Courtship offers two individuals time to discern not merely whether they possess enough shared inter-ests or common goals to make a go of it. More than that, it allows time to discover if they can trust the other's promises as the basis of covenant relationship. The promises of Genesis 9 are by no means bullied or cajoled. They come freely from God to those with whom

God covenants. The promises themselves feed the underlying spirit of grace that permeates this relationship. They thus ground the hope of God's covenant partners in grace. Those promises come down to two assertions. Whether we see hope in them depends on whether we trust the One who speaks them.

The first promise is amazingly simple: "never again." Never again will all flesh be cut off. Never again will a flood destroy the earth. Some of my millennial-oriented friends like to point out here that the promise only pertains to floods. *God didn't say anything about not destroying by fire!* I will not argue with them. If they find it hopeful to see heaven and earth engulfed in fire, then so be it. I would only ask that they (and you) listen closely to the thrice-repeated refrain of God's promise: never again. If "never again" is the starting point and definitive word and not the legalistic loophole of "well, God didn't say nuclear conflagration"—then hope undergirds creation from the outset. Not because it would be nice to think that, but because God has *promised* that.

The second promise grows out of the sign of the rainbow. Notice that in the scripture the bow is not for the sake of Noah. It is for the sake of God. And the bow then begets the second promise God makes to the covenant partners: "I will remember my covenant. . . . I will see it [the bow] and remember the everlasting covenant." The promise is of God's sight and remembrance. The promise avows that we and all creation will not go forgotten.

Now just at this point it is well to ask: do you believe all that? Do you believe, *never again?* Do you believe God sees and remembers? The question is not at all rhetorical. In the darker nights of our souls, in the despairing sights of humankind's inhumanity, the question is not at all rhetorical. It is more than irony that the "never again" spoken by God in the wake of the flood echoed in the "never again" of Jews and others in the wake of Holocaust. In that horrific experience, faithful laments raised up the question of whether God sees and remembers, and if so: why this? We cannot presume that this primal promise of "never again" uttered in Genesis 9 would have been an easy word to hear, much less trust, at the outset. It is still not an easy word to trust. The memory of the ovens of the Third Reich and the killing fields of Cambodia remain awfully close.

To see hope's grounding in grace is not a determination that can be made by those who are merely optimistic. History is far too harsh for faith lightly held. History is far too real for faith to rest content in blissful denial. Faith requires more than naiveté. The biblical witness and the covenant combine trust in the One who promises and action consistent with those promises. If covenant did not rely on the God who promises, then hope would fall on our own shoulders. Works righteousness would be our undoing. If covenant did not evoke action consistent with those promises, then hope would be wishful thinking that left the world and our lives unaffected. Cheap grace would be its delusion. Our hope resides in a covenant grounded in God's grace. God's promises serve not as escape pods from history but as the means for living faithfully within it. Only those who trust "never again" and God's remembrance can endure times when those promises seem long in coming, even longer than our life spans. We do not trust in the times but in God who is our hope.

Grounding in Grace—and the Longing for Home

'Tis grace hath brought me safe thus far, and grace will lead me home.

Fundamental to this entire book, as hinted by its subtitle, is understanding hope's attitude and practice as a longing for home. This is not meant to reduce hope to nostalgia for some past time. Rather, it traces in part to the quote from Saint Augustine on the frontispiece of this book: "You have made us for yourself, and our hearts are restless until they rest in you." Home for the spiritual sojourner involves God's presence. That yearning, that longing to dwell in God's presence is what this book intends by "home." Home is wherever we encounter God, the source of who we are and who we may yet become.

This chapter has sought to lay the framework and foundation of that longing in the grace of God as revealed in the story of God's covenanting with Noah and all creation. This story grounds our hope in grace by reminding us that everywhere we turn, God seeks relationship and offers promises. This covenant asserts we live in an *environment* infused with grace that forms our home and grounds our hope.

So what might that understanding of hope as home feel like? Rev. Lynn Longfield, one of those to whom I turned for perspectives on hope, offered these words. "Home, for me, is the condition or state of knowing not that all *will* be well, but that all *is* well." I believe that sense of home as experienced by Lynn underlies the environment of grace God establishes in covenanting with Noah and all creation. No hope worth holding would deny the elements or experiences in this world that frighten or dehumanize. We do not yet live in the sovereign realm of God. But in the very beginning, at the very foundation, the promises of this covenant confirm that we live with feet firmly planted in grace. "Never again" assures us that God does not have destruction in mind. "I will see . . . and remember" affirms that we will not be forgotten or lost. We may live in this world, upon this earth, among all flesh, and know in our heart of hearts that all is well here. For God is gracious here. This is sanctuary; our feet stand on holy ground, and our faith finds itself grounded in grace. As Lynn has said, home —and you may read there "hope"—is the condition or state of knowing not that all *will* be well, but that all *is* well. Why?

God's covenant is with you and your descendants.
God's covenant is with every living creature on earth.
God's covenant is with the earth.
Never again shall all flesh be cut off.
God will see and remember.
All is well. . . .
If you so hope,
Then so live.

Chapter 2

HOPE

CONFESSING OUR STORY

Deuteronomy 26:1-12

---

*Art was the rememberer. He knew what he knew and
what had been known by a lot of dead kinfolks and neighbors.
They lived on in his mind and spoke there, reminding him
and us of things that needed to be remembered.*
—WENDELL BERRY

If you have not read Wendell Berry, get thee to a library. Beyond his considerable skills as a wordsmith, Berry is a storyteller's storyteller. You do not read his words so much as you hear the accents of his characters' voices and sense the feel of this landscape.

Berry writes the following words on the copyright page of the book from which the opening quote was taken: "This book is a work of fiction. Nothing is in it that has not been imagined." The stories are all made up . . . yet, at the same time, they are all true—true in terms of telling about life, community, and land. They are true to the voices we might hear in such a place where life is lived not by going through the motions but by deep enjoyment and deep grief in its turnings. They are true in a way of peculiar importance in their confession of the connection between hope and community. In the storytelling of Wendell Berry, no solitary individuals live in disconnected places at separate times. All are interwoven. At times the weave is so tight that the boundaries between past and future blur. Characters discover the present's truth in that blurring. Life is never you or I or others alone.

The stories Berry tells, like the character described in the opening quote, remind us of the things that need to be remembered. In doing so Berry writes out of a tradition of stories that stretches all the way back to our faith's beginnings, all the way out to its furthest yearnings, and all the way in to where we live and move today. Such stories confess truth because such stories tell the truth about the ones, and the One, from whom we have come and to whom we belong.

Starting Points

A German book titled *Wittekindsland* documents emigration from the district of Herford in Germany in the 1800s. It contains the following notation (my rough translation from the German): "1859, Jobst Heinrich Indermark, born February 8, 1839." This entry names my great-grandfather. His name appears in the section that lists those who came to the United States without proper consent papers—in today's jargon, as illegal aliens.

As to why my great-grandfather set out on such a journey at risk of being deported upon arrival if discovered by the authorities, the book says nothing. The fact that his name comes in the midst of hundreds of others attests to the truth that he was not alone in this risk-taking journey. My family's oral folklore tells about Anna Ilsabein Indermark, my great-great-grandmother, who packed several of her sons off to America at this time. Why? She didn't want them drafted to fight in the wars of Prussian expansion led by Bismarck. Little did she or her sons know, arriving in St. Louis in the late 1850s, that they would soon be caught up in America's Civil War. When setting out on a new life, there are no guarantees it will be exactly as imagined.

I would like to think that Jobst Heinrich and his family understood from experience the confession in Deuteronomy 26:5 that begins: "A wandering Aramean was my ancestor. . . ." This line falls in the middle of the story narrated by Deuteronomy 26. Why not start at the beginning with the firstfruits and the baskets, with the priest and the altar? Because none of those things makes any sense without this foundational confession. None of those things can be fully under-stood without its story of who I am—which is to say, who we are.

According to the text, the "who" is "a wandering Aramean." That terse description does not engender great expectations. This wander-ing does not correspond to the wandering done these days with vehi-cles towing homes equipped with satellite dish and Italian marble countertops in search of new adventures or warmer climes. This wan-dering corresponds to the state of contemporary folks who have nowhere to call home, no land to afford protection of kin or titled ownership. According to Deuteronomy our story begins with some-one who today resembles the ones lining up in front of a homeless shelter, bending over in a field picking another's crops, or risking a border crossing. That is where and in whom we begin.

Scholars presume that the particular wandering Aramean Deuter-onomy has in mind is Jacob. Jacob, you will remember, is the deceiver who tricked brother Esau out of birthright and father Isaac out of blessing. But the trickery brought him not homeland security but years of flight. Even when homecoming and reconciliation arrived, the wandering did not cease. Jacob, now named Israel, sired and then endured sons who engaged in their own deceptions by bringing home the bloodied coat of son Joseph to deceive the deceiver. Even when news came that Joseph had not died but thrived in Egypt, Jacob did not live out his days in the land promised to Abraham. A famine sent him and offspring wandering to Egypt to be cared for by Joseph. Israel had wandering stamped all over its beginnings—*our* beginnings.

But why speak of this as "our" story and not "his" or "theirs"? The story itself. After verse 5 it leads us into the narrative with the arm's-length shelter of third person singular (*"he* went down into Egypt . . . *he* became a great nation," italics added). Then it suddenly claims us in first person plural: "The Egyptians treated *us* harshly . . . *we* cried . . . the LORD brought *us* out" (italics added). In Deuteronomy 26 we do not overhear somebody else's story. We sit in the living room and hear the eldest family member tell of days and experiences past that have all flowed into who and what and why we are today. Like Berry's character Art, Deuteronomy 26 knows and confesses the things that need to be remembered. Like the dead who live in Art's mind and who speak through his stories, our confession begins with a wandering Aramean who is vulnerable, at risk. One for whom land and home and hope will come, if they are to come at all, as gift entrusted for stewardship rather than right claimed by ownership.

This is a curious starting point for confessing our story and a necessary one. It is curious in that it flies in the face of narratives extolling heritage, religious or otherwise, as stamped with "bound to succeed" because of some innate ability to pull ourselves up by our own bootstraps. No such guarantees attach to the sort of wanderers we meet in Deuteronomy. Its story guarantees that ours will be a narrative of grace. It delivers us from strivings driven by race or nation or even religion to assert claims of pedigree that make me and mine superior to you and yours.

Our starting point in a wandering Aramean also provides an apt metaphor for what life continues to be for us. We are all wanderers. No matter the outward trappings of our economics or community setting, no matter our political inclinations or Myers-Briggs aptitudes, we are all on a journey. The question is *how* will we journey? The first half of Jacob's story might have made it seem as if wanderers live only by their wits and cunning. But by story's end—and this confession's beginning—it becomes clear that wanderers rely on the grace of God and the kindness of others. Grace and kindness may not always be evident along the way. In those times, hope earns its keep. My friend and writing colleague Jan Seale frames the connection between hope and journey this way:

> I hardly ever think of hope as a destination or a resting place. I see it as a conscious enactment on a journey, and, for me, in good times the journey is all I can know (or maybe even care about).

We are on a journey begun by a wandering Aramean. But "he" and the "we" who emerge from that story are not the only ones who travel this way. An Other intrudes at the story's core.

The Intruding God

We have sometimes become quite comfortable conversing about God in the third person in congregations and denominational gatherings and intramural creedal debates. We intone our various beliefs and air our even more various differences about God the way we occasionally speak across a hospital bed with other visitors to the exclusion of the patient who is our alleged concern. It seems as if our enlightened faith tries to make up for a God who has become a silent partner, uninvolved in the daily affairs now solely in our hands. As a result we may raise our eyebrows and lower our esteem in the direction of those who speak of God's acting in our midst in our day.

Skepticism of such claims of divine intrusion among us is often well-founded. For many individuals and communities, the claimed intrusion of God seems to have an uncanny tendency to further the ambitions and line the pockets of the claimant. When I recall the visions of Jesus announced by Oral Roberts in the 1980s, linked by him to the raising of funds for his ministry—I get skeptical. I have doubts about the "God with us" rhetoric that in times past and present has furthered self-righteous violence and self-serving national policies. But healthy skepticism is a tool of faith, not its replacement.

Over the years I have also become more open to the possibility of God's intrusions. Occasionally in my pastoral work a person would disclose an experience for which the only proper term is *mystical*. I too have had moments when it seemed God intruded in my life or the life of a loved one in comforting and even saving ways. Granted, such experiences have been a far cry from divine intervention on behalf of peoples and nations. However, faith's openness to God's intruding among us does have to start somewhere. So was I or those others only projecting hopes into events that can be explained otherwise? Reluctance to embrace such stories may arise out of our perception of the individual doing the telling. But on a deeper level, reluctance may stem from a difficulty in perceiving God as intruding in any such ways. What is your experience?

My own experiences and those of others push me to take seriously stories like the one that begins with a wandering Aramean and his descendants. When that story reaches its flash point in Egypt, a new character takes center stage and carries the action. In verses 7-9 of Deuteronomy 26, God takes every decisive action. God hears, God sees, God brings out, God brings in, God gives. In other words, God intrudes.

This is not the sort of intrusion that parallels help in finding car keys slipped down between the sofa cushions. It is even further from the help attested by victors in sporting events where Jesus is duly thanked for the winning drive and the final score. This story, confessed to be our story, proclaims God's intrusion into history and society on behalf of at-risk people and against prevailing powers. The confession of the Deuteronomist here does not speculate on philosophical attributes of divine being, nor does it finesse doctrinal fine points to weed out the "real" believers (usually us). This story confesses divine action that intercedes in human affairs: bringing down the pharaohs for the sake of lowly ones. Do you believe that God intercedes for the vulnerable? And more to the point of this book: do you hope that?

We find ourselves at this juncture in the realm of what Søren Kierkegaard once spoke of as the "leap of faith." In my biased perspective, I do not believe God's intrusions are patently obvious, so disagreement or debate is impossible. Read the accounts of Israel in Egypt and then the wilderness. You get the distinct impression that God's intrusion was not perceived with anywhere near unanimous consent. Lots of folks grumbled. Not a few voiced preference for the good old days, when at least they got their bellies full in Egypt. It becomes easier in hindsight to label this or that event as moved by God's hand, especially when the event has the weight of scriptured word behind it. But what of now? All kinds of events have been heralded as the results of God's working in history: the establishment of the state of Israel in the wake of Holocaust, the end of apartheid. Those developments were by no means "unanimous consent" in terms of attributions to God's intervention or purposes.

Short of having CNN's live feed from some place of crisis interrupted by the voice of God declaring, "Hello, this is my doing here!" we go by faith. We go by what we have experienced of God in word and community, in sacrament and in neighbor. We go in hope that God's actions on behalf of what is good did not end with the Exodus or Jesus' ministry but continue here and now among us. Sometimes, if not most of the time, we go in hope that God's working occurs through human agents. The church's identification as the body of Christ is one major hint about the truth of God's working through ordinary people. That such diverse individuals fill the biblical stories affirms that same truth. Rahab and Moses, Jesus and Magdalene, unnamed Samaritans and unheralded women: the cast of characters is part of the story and part of the leap of faith. Who would think God would work through the likes of . . . (you fill in the blank with the least likely and most surprising to your sensibilities).

Perhaps we find it more difficult to consider particular human agents through whom God works among us than it is to concede God's direct intervention in the historical process. Either way, the story we confess as ours in Deuteronomy 26 compels us to consider the hopeful possibility that God still intrudes. But this intrusion does not negate our responsibility as human beings to work for a just and compassionate world, as if God will "fix" everything if we just sit back and wait long enough. If anything, God's intrusion cements the motivation and vision for our responsibility.

This chapter earlier made the point of how the story of a wandering Aramean became our story. Words about what happened to "him" became words about what happened to "us." But now, in the wake of God's decisive action on our behalf, the text makes another shift. Because of God, the story and its hope do not end with "us." The story of God's redemptive action for "us" now turns to "you." Beyond that, it closes by calling "you" to bring hospitality and justice to "others," whose lot in life bears striking resemblance to the story's start in a wanderer.

Confession Enacted: Hospitality and Justice

Millions is a movie about a boy who has a large sum of money literally fall out of the sky, or so it seemed, and into his lap. He takes his older brother into his confidence. Soon the older boy is devising ways to buy friends and be cool at their new school. The young boy, whose fascination with saints comes through in delightful visionary encounters, has other ideas. He wants to give the money to the poor, whom he sets off to find, for he sees all as a gift from God.

The movie is a fantasy . . . or is it? Listen to how Deuteronomy 26 poses the story. The recitation of God's saving deeds culminates in the gift of a land "flowing with milk and honey." More than that, the land produces very real harvests, and its tangible fruits now come into play in this liturgy that brackets the confession of what God has done. God's blessings have flowed. The land has produced. Now comes the question: what will you do in return? When this land and its bounty fall into your lap as a gifts from above, what will you do with the gifts?

The ritual of firstfruits takes place at a sanctuary. Initially, it sounds like an authorization for religious institutions everywhere and at all times afterward to receive a morning offering. But neither the text nor its ritual of offering ends with ingathering. "Then" verse 11 begins— then such grace as God exercised in raising up a community out of at-risk wanderers now goes exercised by that same community toward other at-risk wanderers among them: Levites, aliens, widows, orphans. The celebration of God's "good," the literal meaning of "bounty" in verse 11, is to be shared with the vulnerable ones among us. The gifts of harvest are to be given away so others may eat. Firstfruits gathered into holy places become firstfruits sent out for holy uses.

Every one of the groups mentioned in verses 11-12 lived at risk. The Levites were the one tribal group in Israel who had no land to harvest and support themselves. Aliens were landless foreigners in Israel who did not even have the protection afforded by kinship. Widows and orphans traditionally had no source of support except for the charity of the community. Together, all relied on the hospitality of the community. Together, all relied on acts of justice on their behalf. Denied either, survival was at risk. Provided both, hope was possible.

Deuteronomy's ritual is an act of radical hope that acknowledges life and harvest as God's gracious gifts. The good we enjoy is not ours to grasp or hoard for fear of losing. The good we enjoy becomes the means of enlarging the circle of those who experience and confess life's source in God. The ritual summons actions from us that give hope to those who otherwise might live without it.

When we claim this story as our own and in turn find ourselves claimed by it, the story reminds us of things that need to be remembered. It reminds the institutional church that gatherings of offerings and drives for support—and the motivations invoked for either—need connection to hospitality and justice. Enrichment or prestige of the sanctuary, whether envisioned in steepled buildings or denominational structures, is not the point of the ritual. The point is celebration of the bounty and the sharing of its good with the most vulnerable. The point is community.

Notice the wording in verse 11: *"together with* the Levites and the aliens"* (italics added). Sometimes our offerings and actions, even in the name of justice, keep folks at arm's length. We try to do good for others but shy away from direct contact. Yet our vocation is less about doling out charity to deserving strangers than it is a call to welcome at-risk strangers into community. We give them a place with us . . . and within the story that has graciously embraced us. Another storied remembrance about God and God's community tells us:

> For the LORD your God is God of gods and Lord of lords, the great God, mighty and awesome, who is not partial and takes no bribe, who executes justice for the orphan and the widow, and who loves the strangers, providing them food and clothing. You shall also love the stranger, for you were strangers in the land of Egypt (Deut. 10:17-19).

Confessing Our Story—and the Longing for Home

The best stories enable us to hear ourselves within them and find our place through them. The best storytellers fashion words that draw us into the narrative and send us out again changed and transformed.

Deuteronomy 26 begins as a story told of ancient peoples and unfamiliar practices. Yet the word *wandering* brings connection. We recall times and places in our lives when we have been that wandering one. Once we identify with the wanderer of this confession, we find ourselves invited into community with other sojourners and into recognition of God's gracious intrusion on our behalf. A distant story becomes a hopeful story, for we understand it brings us good news that we long to hear. It brings us to a place we long to be. With others. With God. In the confession of this story and others like it, we find ourselves and are found in what is home to us. Yet even then the story does not close or let us go. In its reaching out to us it evokes our reaching out to others with its gift of place and its meeting of needs. This story brings "home" out of the realm of cozied private shelters into the providing of sanctuary for vulnerable ones who face danger. This story brings hope out of the naive optimism that "every day in every way things are getting better" into the vocation of trusting God and doing justice and extending welcome. Why? As the story tells it: this is the way of God, and we are the people of God.

All of this begins with our ability to hear ourselves named in the story of a wanderer and then to trust God's care that embraces us and every wanderer before and after. For God loves sojourners. God loves the very ones we find it hardest to accept, including at times ourselves.

We need to remember such things when the amnesia of privilege threatens to undo community by saying it belongs to those who have earned it rather than those who need it. We bear them in mind when the fog of exclusion threatens to usurp community by daring to delineate God's grace with the borders of our intolerances. We recall them when the forgetfulness of our generation threatens to constrict community by thinking the church has only been—and can only be—as we have known it. We celebrate our origins in wanderers, in gracious deliverance, in a calling to share God's good.

We are still on journey and are still in need of grace. God still calls us to stewardship that is less about institutional maintenance and more about celebrating God's good with others.

Remember these things.
They tell your story.
They speak your hope.
They form your home.
You, and every beloved child of God.

Chapter 3

HOPE

TRUSTING GOD'S LEADING

Psalm 23

As I live among the farmers of the Red River Valley, I sense a confidence that God will provide and that care of God's creation will yield food for all. In spite of the vagaries of weather and markets, each spring their hearts swell with fresh hope, and they plant another crop.

—REBECCA GROTHE

Follow the leader is a game we play as children. All follow the steps or imitate the motions of the designated one. The game involves significant trust. Will the leader be trusted not to walk the followers into some place of danger? Will the leader be trusted not to call for movements or actions that would make all look foolish in their repetition? Trust is a commodity whose exchange between us is not automatic. It must be given rather than demanded. It must be earned, not coerced. We shy away from those who expend time asking for our trust, for trust grows, if at all, out of experience that manifests reliability and care.

Hope relies on trust. Trust in the dependability of a friend begets hope that she will act on your behalf and for your good. Trust in the rhythm of nature and God's providence engenders such hope as that which Rebecca identifies in the opening quote. And trust in the leading of God gives birth to the hope that permeates Psalm 23, the Shepherd Psalm. Unlike some passages of scripture that seem unfamiliar to the terrain of our lives, the words of Psalm 23 sound like the voice of a beloved and well-acquainted companion. These words have traveled with many from the earliest years of faith's journey. Yet it is not its familiarity that causes us to consider this psalm now. It is the psalm's powerful and surprising affirmations about the consequences of following the God confessed as shepherd by the psalmist and by us. "The Lord is my shepherd." Where might such leading take us?

Why Do I Want?

Isn't that a misprint? Shouldn't it read "what do I want"? After all, our culture encourages people to "want" all manner of things. Consumerism continually drives us to redefine and expand the list of "what I want." Items that our grandparents and even parents would have considered inconceivable luxuries have become absolute necessities today. Can you imagine telling people forty years ago that they really *needed* to have a telephone cinched to their belt to stay in touch?

I italicized the word in the previous sentence for a reason. In our language and values, we sometimes fail to distinguish between wants and needs. When the distinction between the two blurs, we lose perspective on life's requirements. That loss of perspective makes it imperative to substitute *why* for *what* in the opening question raised about wants. The imperative to do so comes from our faith and also from this psalm.

Listen to this extraordinary claim tucked unobtrusively in the second half of the first verse: "I shall not want." The Hebrew word translated as "want" literally means "to lack." At this point the psalm's familiarity may work against our fully hearing its message. Think of all the times you have heard or recited this psalm. You have heard and said, "I shall not want." Really? If we speak of wants or "lacking" as does the surrounding culture, this verse is nonsense. Not to want cuts against the grain of what we are *encouraged* to do. Want also suffers from a peculiar disorder related to the confusion of wants and needs. "Want" has become a euphemism in our time for those who exist in poverty. The poor live in want, we solemnly say. I believe the poor live in need; the rest of us live in want.

Want, in our use of the word, has become a synonym for unfettered desire. The problem is that language accustoms us to acting. When we do not distinguish between need and want in our speech, we are much more liable to fail to make that distinction in our living. The price paid for that failure in our values and in community can be devastating. It has long been that way. The New Testament epistle of James addresses this issue in graphic terms:

> Those conflicts and disputes among you, where do they come from? Do they not come from your cravings that are at war within you? You want something and do not have it; so you commit murder. And you covet something and cannot obtain it; so you engage in disputes and conflicts (4:2).

James does not write here of an economic crisis; he writes of a spiritual crisis generated by the failure to distinguish between wants and needs. The text's use of the word *covet* calls to mind ancient warnings about not letting wants race ahead of judgment and values. War and murder, disputes and conflicts: in such terms James makes clear the devastation set loose when wants and coveting reign supreme.

Psalm 23 confronts this attitude with the scandalous teaching that those who trust God's leading do not have to be tied into the cravings of materialism. The "shall" of "I shall not want" implies a decision on our part, a decision to live in a way contrary to the cycle of wanting and coveting described by James. "I shall not want" confesses that God's leading will supply us with what we truly need for life. God's leading does not take form in competition with the secular world to see who is better at obtaining our wish lists. Don't let some of those televised ministry shows fool you: the ones where gilded chairs and red velvet curtains and glittering jewelry abound; the ones where affluence has undergone the theological equivalent of cosmetic surgery to give it the appearance of Christian virtue. Baptize it the "health and wealth" gospel. Christen it the "name it and claim it" gospel. Embellish it with another faith title. But greed is greed, no matter whose name is evoked. Gaudy displays of wealth do not banish wants. They only feed them. Wants lose their power to seduce us in the trust of God's leading.

That is the assertion of Psalm 23. An equally clear affirmation comes in this insight into the wilderness sojourn of Israel made by Deuteronomy 2:7: "These forty years the LORD your God has been with you; you have *lacked nothing*," (emphasis added). The verb used there is the same as in Psalm 23:1: "I shall not want." God's presence promises the lack of nothing that we truly need. Granted, there may be a world of difference between the lack of nothing we truly need and what we say we want or think we need. But the psalm invites us to the discipline of trust. To trust God in such a way that wants are seen for what they truly are—and what they are not. To trust God in such a way that we find ourselves freed from the spiraling cycle of always wanting more and more, only to grow less and less satisfied. To trust God in such a way that, with what we have, we share with those who truly *do* live in need—and to know we are richer, not poorer, for doing so. Such trust in God's leading unleashes hope for a new way of living responsibly and joyfully in this world as we discover the psalmist's experience to be our own: I shall not want.

A life free of wanting, however, does not come out of nowhere. We cannot will or achieve this life on our own, much less at the expense of others. Such a life comes by entrusting our lives to the holy presence of God, whose care would enfold and lead all.

Trusting in Holy Presence

What does it mean to live in the midst of holy presence, a presence we trust with our lives and well-being? Lynn Longfield offers this experience from her childhood in which she recognizes life lived in holy presence.

> When I was a very little girl, if older children were teasing me on my way home from school or a dog seemed ready to menace me or some anxiety or worry or fear plagued me, a warm relief would envelop my

mind, body, and spirit once the back door opened wide and I stepped inside our familiar kitchen. I was home.

Imagine stepping through that door. You feel safe, warm, loved, home. Think of when and where you have had such an experience in your relationship with God. Perhaps it was only a momentary glimpse of standing on sacred ground, graced with holy presence. This psalm promises that such presence is with us always, everywhere, whether we are aware of it or not. And in such holy presence, we are invited, like Lynn, to find ourselves "at home."

Such a sense of place, such a recognition of holy presence surrounds the psalmist. We see that suggested by the way the psalm is put together. The holy name of God (*YHWH*), revealed to Moses at the burning bush and left unpronounced by devout Jews, occurs in the opening and closing verses of this psalm. Everything in between is bracketed by the Holy One. Even all of the first-person pronoun references ("I, me, my") that recur throughout this psalm do not fall prey to a self-centered view of life. Every reference to "I, me, my" connects to a corresponding assertion of what God does. *I* will fear no evil because of the close presence of God. God restores *my* soul. God leads *me* beside still waters. The focus remains on God. In whatever situation we enter, God may be trusted as One who will meet our genuine needs—which are again not necessarily our pressing wants.

To further convey this sense of our being enfolded within holy presence, the psalm uses the image of God as shepherd. In Hebrew the root word of shepherd means "to feed." A shepherd is one who feeds, who provides what is needed for life. Consider that meaning in light of the psalm's depictions of God's shepherding. "Green pastures" nourish the flock. "Still waters" offer drink. God brings rest. God's shepherding nurtures us with what makes for life. Isaiah 40:11 also invokes the image of God as shepherd. There, God as shepherd takes lambs in arm and gently leads the mother sheep. The two passages together depict God's shepherding in tender and nurturing ways. In our time we often only focus on shepherding's associations with gentle nurture.

But shepherding also includes companioning through danger and tough work done in trying conditions. Jewish scriptures frequently use shepherding as an image for kingship and sovereignty.

That association of shepherds with rulers in Judaism goes far beyond how a shepherd boy named David came to be anointed king. The prophets identified Israel's and Judah's kings as shepherds. The shepherds' chief calling was to rule in such a way that provided for the "flock" entrusted to their care. As Ezekiel and others point out, Israel's shepherds often failed in that vocation. The first line of Psalm 23 affirms both God as shepherd and the psalmist as one who confirms loyalty: "The LORD is *my* shepherd." In those words, the psalmist asserts a political as well as a religious truth. To confess God as shepherd is to confess allegiance to God's authority, which surpasses all other authorities. God's shepherding stands not only for comforting care but also conveys trust in and encourages action on behalf of God's sovereign reign.

As a result, "the Lord is my shepherd" can become a subversive word among us. Such potential arises when temporal authorities claim for themselves blind or unlimited allegiance. Such potential emerges when lesser shepherds make demands that deny or undermine the qualities of God's realm such as justice and compassion. The Shepherd Psalm acknowledges One and only One as sovereign in creation. "The Lord is my shepherd" provides both starting point and summons to responsible participation—and dissent when necessary—in the body politic. We exercise participation and dissent with humility, not claiming exclusive access to the mind of God, and we exercise these aspects with courage, knowing ourselves and all creation as claimed by God.

Shepherding in Israel symbolized the use of power for the sake of community and in particular for those most vulnerable. That remains true today. For that reason, the psalm's theme and model of shepherding extends not just to the "big picture" items of national and societal relationships as indicated in the previous paragraph. It also includes the tighter spheres of where you and I exercise the powers we pos-

sess. It does us or faith little good to rail against the abuses of shepherds on the world arena, when closer to home we neglect vulnerable ones. To live in the holy presence of God and to trust God as
shepherd means we are open to transformation in the way we live and
shepherd those under our care. As parents. As children who become
caregivers for parents. As participants in community and congregation and family. "The Lord is *my* shepherd" invokes trust of holy presence. And God's presence intends to transform for the good the ways
in which we engage in all those relationships.

But what happens when "for the good" seems long delayed if not
denied? What happens when the world around us and within us turns
for the worse rather than the better? Where is hope then? For that, we
must move with the psalm into the face of fear, into valleys whose
shadows we dread entering.

Even Though . . .

One memorable exchange in the *The Fellowship of the Ring*, the first
book in The Lord of the Rings trilogy, involves Frodo the bearer of
the ring and Gandalf the wizard. Frodo wishes that things had turned
out otherwise. Gandalf responds, "So do all who live to see such
times. But that is not for them to decide. All we have to decide is what
to do with the time that is given to us."[1] There are many times in our
lives we would not have chosen, had the choice been ours. A doctor
solemnly intones the C word as diagnosis. A friend calls from inside
the ambulance that is transporting your son. A television set is turned
on, just in time to watch the image of a second plane flying into a
building. When such times confront us, such times as the psalmist
envisions in valleys with death-cast shadows: what makes it possible
to say that fear will not own the day?

"You are with me." You. It may seem odd, easily overlooked—but
this is the first time the psalmist speaks directly to God. The opening
verses form a beautiful litany of God's shepherding care. They are
liturgical, like a responsive reading or an affirmation of faith. They are

about God, and there is nothing wrong with that. But when the psalm enters that place where shadows chill and disorient, the celebration of God in third-person language ("he") changes to address of God in the second person. *You* are with me.

We often speak of God in the third person: "I believe this about God," or "I hope God will do that." Creeds take that form of address. It can be helpful to use third person when we are describing our understandings of God or engaging in dialogue with others about those beliefs. At some point, though, faith must become direct address: spoken, prayed, praised in the second person. If faith is to penetrate into our spirit and bones, "God is with me [us]" must be experienced as "You are with me [us]."

But how does the presence of another, even if that Other is God, make it possible to dispense with fear? On the one hand, we have experiences of the power of human presence to alleviate, if not dispel, fear. Children are readily open to the comfort brought by another's presence. No parents worth their salt would let a child go to a doctor's appointment alone! Sometimes we think maturity and adulthood means having to let go of such reassuring presence. We're grown-up, you know. But in my pastoral ministry, I recall few people who relished being alone in the face of some family crisis or impending surgery. There remains something comforting, even empowering, in companionship during difficult times. That remains true when the crisis involves engaging in public words or action for which opposition is clear. Voice and resolve are strengthened when we know we do not stand alone.

Such experiences may help us understand why the psalmist's "You are with me" can banish fear. But only to a point. Trusting God to be with us—and for us—moves beyond the support afforded by human companionship. Why and how that is finds witness in a pair of words the psalmist uses in reference to the presence God brings: "rod" and "staff." They may seem like synonyms, but they are not.

"Staff" clearly invokes the psalm's image of God as shepherd. Such staffs typically were long wooden sticks with a crooked handle.

Some church traditions to this day use staffs as the sign of the office of bishop. A shepherd's staff, however, was not ceremonial. The staff served as a walking stick for the shepherd, especially useful in scrambling up rocky hillsides. It might also be assumed that the staff served as the shepherd's—and therefore the flock's—primary defense against predators. It was not. For those situations, shepherds used a slingshot to ward off threats from a distance or a wooden club imbedded with sharpened bits of metal for confrontations close at hand. So what might the psalm have in mind for the "comfort" provided by a staff? The bend at the handle served as a means to lift sheep out of danger. Most of all, the shepherd used the staff to guide the sheep along the way or into the sheepfold. "Comfort" came in rescue and guidance.

Consider that in the light of our own experiences of God. We come to know God in gracious acceptance. We are not left alone to extricate ourselves from situations we have fallen or walked blindly into that put relationship with God at peril. God seeks us out. Ours is the comfort of a God who reaches out to us in forgiveness. Ours is also the comfort of knowing God as guide, a comfort experienced when we entrust ourselves to God's leading.

In addition to the staff, the psalmist also speaks of a "rod" that brings comfort. As J. Clinton McCann Jr. notes in his comments on this psalm in *The New Interpreter's Bible*, this word "even more frequently signifies royal authority and rule." To speak of the comfort brought by this rod is to return to the identification of God's shepherding with God's sovereignty. Where is the comfort or hope in that? Creation, history, your life and mine: all that has been and is now and ever will be, belong to God. The powers that threaten to destroy life and deny hope do not have the last word. There is a limit to how far they may go and how wide they may reach. That limit is imposed by God: by God's love, by God's justice, by God's realm. The exercise of faith in the face of those powers bears witness in word and deed to that truth, even and especially when it seems those powers have their way in our time. The exercise of faith in the face of those powers says with the psalmist: "I fear no evil."

I fear no evil. That is not bravado or foolhardiness. That is not an assertion willed up out of our psychological strength or physical might. Fear is not banished by what we possess, whether in weaponry or bank accounts. Fear is banished by who stands by us, the One who is Shepherd. Fear ends and faith begins with the spoken and lived confession: "You are with me."

Trusting God's Lead—and the Longing for Home

The image of God as shepherd brings a multitude of insights to faith. Some have been the focus of this chapter's explorations. The shepherd is one who leads. The life of faith follows God's leading. Following relies on our trust of the One who is shepherd.

But what has all of this to do with the notion of home and hope as its longing? By dwelling on the image of God as shepherd, Psalm 23 intimates our "home" to be in the presence of the Shepherd. And shepherds are notorious for movement. That is their job: to move the flock to fresh pastures and safe places. God also maintains a notorious penchant for movement. God moved with Israel into Egypt and back to a once-promised land to bring life. The prophets argued that God moved in the experience of exile and then in return. The faithful ones in both cases were not those who dug in heels and said God is here and nowhere else. The faithful ones experienced God on the way, within the guidance, through the deliverance. The Incarnation might even be considered the ultimate expression of God's movement: to stand with us, to know death in order to resurrect life. Our home is God's presence, and God's presence is on the move.

The Shepherd Psalm reveals we are a pilgrim people. It reveals God to be a shepherding God: guiding, delivering, leading, empowering us with holy presence. How we engage in that pilgrimage, how we find ourselves at home on the way invites our trust. The psalm invites us to live faith not in third-person descriptions of God but in second-person prayer and hope toward God. So, in closing, listen to the Shepherd Psalm, offered as a pilgrim's prayer.

You are the One who shepherds,
   who transforms wanting ones into grateful ones.
You are the One who restores,
   who gives rest and food and drink.
You are the One who leads,
   and whose leading is for good.
You are the One who companions in brightness and shadow,
   who seeks out wanderers and reigns in power.
You are the One who welcomes.
   You are the One who is home.
You at beginning, You at ending,
   You at all times and places between and beyond.
                    You.

Chapter 4

HOPE

RESTORING JUSTICE

Isaiah 65:17-25

---

*I think eternal life gives the broken and the impaired and
those whose lives have been destroyed space and time
and strength to live the life which they were intended for. . . .
I think it for the sake of the justice which I believe is
God's concern and . . . first option.*

—JÜRGEN MOLTMANN

I don't remember meeting Danielle, though I'm sure I saw her at
games at the high school or Downriver Days celebrations held each
July in Ione. Danielle lived on a farm outside of town with her parents
and brothers and sister. Her life was filled with school activities and
Girl Scout programs. Most of all, Danielle loved horses. She even had
one of her own to ride and enjoy.

I received the call on a Saturday. Danielle and a friend had been
playing in the pasture. Apparently Danielle ran behind her horse, and
it flicked up one of its back hooves. Others later said that an inch of
difference in where it struck would have changed the outcome: a broken nose, a fractured jaw, shattered teeth but no more. But the hoof
caught her at just the wrong spot. It broke her neck, and she died
instantly, six months shy of her thirteenth birthday. Imagine gathering with that family and hundreds of others at the graveside on Monday. What would you want to say about where God is or is not, about
what God "wills" in such events? Or, to raise the issue that drives this
chapter: what would you say, could you say, about justice?

We normally view justice as right and equitable relationships in society. It is that, and this chapter will explore how hope figures in the restoration of justice in the face of social inequities. But justice is also about fairness in the way life plays out—or ceases to be—independent of individual choices or societal structures. The opening quote from Jürgen Moltmann places that primal issue of fairness on God's shoulders. What might the justice of God mean for Danielle or others like her? What basis might we have for hope in the restoration of such justice? "I am about to create new heavens and a new earth."

Life Is Not Fair

This expression is probably familiar to most parents and even more so to children. The learning of life's unfairness is a prerequisite for open-eyed entrance into job markets, school competitions, and all manner of enterprises. Unfortunately, the adoption of *life is not fair* as the core truth of human existence ultimately creates not realism but apathy, and worse. For if unfairness, inequity, or injustice is life's bottom line and all we can expect, what motivates us to live fairly, equitably, or justly? *Life is not fair* may harden us against inevitable disappointments, but *life is not fair* does not possess any hope for transforming those inequities. At best it prepares us to absorb them. At worst it sets us up to inflict them.

The people originally addressed by Isaiah 65:17-25 had good reason to consider life as not fair. They were, by one dating of the material, the community of Israel exiled in Babylon. Many would have been children, not even born at the time when exile began. Through no fault of their own, they had captivity levied upon them. Life was not fair. Others consider the group addressed by Isaiah 65 to be the community of Israel restored to their homeland by the Persians under Cyrus. But the homecoming had not turned out to be what some had seemingly promised it to be. The rebuilding of Jerusalem, even just a rudimentary wall for protection, proved to be a trying task. Neighbors sabotaged rather than assisted the efforts. Through no fault of their own, the returnees found existence in some ways more difficult than in captivity. Life was not fair.

When a community reaches consensus that life is not fair, then or now, a crisis occurs that requires a choice. Do we accept life's unfairness as the way things are, sometimes resigning ourselves to inequities, or do we decide to contest that consensus and live otherwise? Rather than limit this conversation to sixth-century Israel, let us observe a more recent crisis—and choice.

September 11, 2001

The families and friends of the nearly three thousand fatalities of that day and countless thousands more injured in body or spirit have absolute justification to assert life's unfairness. Parents, partners, and children who had gone to work or gotten on planes or responded as police and fire personnel did nothing to bring this on themselves. By reason of vocation, coincidence, or courage, they were at the wrong place at the wrong time—though by all rights they had no cause to think otherwise. For them, in that instance, life was utterly and tragically not fair. The world joined this nation in mourning those dead and grieving that unfairness.

But as noted before, when a community concedes that life is not fair, a crisis of choice looms. One choice includes adoption of inequity as a fact of life. From there, it is not a huge ethical jump to accepting inequities in our response and retaliation. Abu Ghraib. The suspension of civil rights for uncharged suspects. The protections of the Geneva Convention set aside as obsolete in contemporary times. *Hey, life is not fair. We're just giving back what we got. Why should our responses be burdened by the limiting issue of the justice of such acts?*

Why? "I am about to create new heavens and a new earth." The community formed by the words and vision of Isaiah, then and now, understands that how things have been does not cement how they must always be. The hope shaped by these words asserts that life's unfairness does not lock us into inescapable destiny, much less absolve a tit-for-tat ethic. Isaiah's witness moves justice from a tenet of faith about God's realm beyond time into an embodiment of faithfulness to God in the midst of history.

"I am about to create new heavens and a new earth." To say that life is not fair is old news. It states the obvious. But the way out of the old and obvious comes in Isaiah's promise of the "new": new heavens, new earth. Other prophets also anticipated that hope would have to make a decisive break with the past. While Isaiah states the "new" in creation terms, others addressed the need for and promise of newness in other ways. Ezekiel invited a turning to God's ways through the gift of a new spirit and heart (18:31). For Jeremiah the new came in relational terms: "I [God] will make a *new* covenant with the house of Israel and the house of Judah" (31:31, italics added). New heart. New spirit. New covenant. Coupled with new heavens and new earth, hope invites openness to venture into uncharted territory both without and within.

That invitation to the new can make hope difficult. Embrace of the new does not come easily, at least to those of us (and I am one) who value tradition and precedent. Sometimes the difficulty arises from resistance to the unknown—as in, better the devil we know than the one we don't know. Sometimes, the difficulty comes from not perceiving that life can be any other way. This latter hurdle seems more the case with unfairness. It's not that we prefer life to be unfair. We just cannot conceive of things being any other way than the way they are.

Faith says that the new is possible. We have it on good authority (Isaiah 65:17-25) that the order of this world is about to undergo a dramatic reversal. Hope then becomes more than just wishing it were so and sooner than later. Hope takes that promise of newness and applies it to the present conduct of our lives. Hope insists that justice is more than pie in the sky: it is the purpose of God for life lived now in anticipation of its fulfillment. Hope does not usurp the responsibility to establish justice from the hands of God. But neither does hope abdicate our responsibility as those called of God to live in concert with what faith reveals as God's future.

What does that future consist of that might provide hints and clues to our present witness and faithfulness? I understand the importance of not dwelling on negatives. But to speak of the hope of God's justice restored is, among other things, to say: "No more!"

No More

Key turning points in history toward justice have often begun with a refusal to accept injustice as the way things are and thus must be. Two different stories assert this "no more."

In the early fifth century, a Christian monk named Telemachus made pilgrimage from Asia Minor to Rome. On arrival he followed crowds that led to a stadium where gladiatorial contests were underway. Appalled at the sight of the violence, Telemachus made his way onto the field and sought to intervene between two of the combatants. His action infuriated the crowd, whose entertainment had been interrupted. Some picked up stones and rained them down on the monk until he lay dead. Some traditions hold that Emperor Honorius heard of the outrage, others that he himself witnessed it. In any event, he issued a decree shortly thereafter that banned such contests. After Telemachus, gladiator contests were no more.

On Thursday, December 1, 1955, a forty-two-year-old African-American seamstress got on a bus to go home after work. She walked past the "Whites Only" rows and found an empty seat in the middle of the bus. As long as such seats were unneeded by whites, she did not need to go to the "colored only"section at the back of the bus. After a couple of more stops, however, the bus filled. The bus driver told the folks in her row, all black, to get up and go to the back of the bus. No one moved. He ordered them to do so a second time. Everyone but the seamstress obeyed. She remained seated. The driver then got up, walked back to where she sat, and told her to move. She said no. He left the bus and brought back a policeman, who arrested Rosa Parks. Segregation, Jim Crow laws, and racial discrimination did not end with Mother Parks' witness on that day. We still have a ways to go on this issue. But where we are now is not where we were in December of 1955. Rosa Parks' simple determination became a watershed moment for a movement that would insist on "no more" for such things.

I doubt that either of the central characters in those two stories had Isaiah 65 clearly in mind when they did what they did. But I do not doubt that the determination and hope behind this passage resonated in their decisions to say and act in the spirit of "no more" in the face of these injustices. Such stories and others like them help us translate this passage from words about hope into hope that is lived out. These words seek and can find embodiment when individuals and communities willingly risk the tenets of faith in the practice of discipleship. Hope is more than an expectant attitude we carry. Hope's expectation of God's good purposes intends to shape what we do and say now that embodies, however tentatively, the qualities and promises of God's realm.

Isaiah's "no more" focuses on two vexing experiences in human existence: the frailty of life at its beginning and at its end. "No more shall there be in it an infant that lives but a few days, or an old person who does not live out a lifetime" (65:20). This chapter's opening story about Danielle poses one aspect of life ended too soon. Parents of SIDS (Sudden Infant Death Syndrome) victims can give eloquent testimony to the tragedy of life cut short. Yet another witness comes in the countless faces we see when a news team finds its way to the latest world crisis of famine or refugees. We see images of children who do not have the energy to brush the flies off their face, the spindly legs and bloated bellies of those who will likely not finish the year, if even the day. We may perceive that even the ones who do survive face enormous odds against ever knowing anything but want and deprivation. We see them, and then we see our children and those of our neighbors: same age, same human spirit. And we wonder why? Why does one know plenty, and the other suffer only lack? If God is just, why? Isaiah promises: no more!

At the other end of the spectrum, Isaiah's "no more" sounds against the hollowness many elders experience. "Live out a lifetime" in verse

20 literally means, according to one translator of that Hebrew phrase, "fill the days." There can be a world of difference at the close of life between days that are filled and days that are simply passed—or days that pass without any seeming awareness of them. My mother's twelve-year descent into Alzheimer's disease shapes my hearing of this text in a very particular way. The knowledge that she was far from alone in that experience does not bring comfort. It only sharpens the question of life's fairness. If God is just, then her end and others like hers, cannot be the end. Hope comes in the form of: no more!

But is "no more" only a wish for what will come at history's end for such as these? God forbid. Isaiah's vision, Isaiah's hope of "no more" serves as a call to arms to do all in our power to change such destinies. If it does not, we make a mockery of these words. If it does not, we ignore the possibility that God calls us to be the ones who begin to turn the tide toward "no more" in our day as a sign of that coming realm's promise. Hope is meant to energize the faithful in this present, not anesthetize us to this day's sufferings and enigmas.

Does that mean it is within our power to fulfill Isaiah's vision of what shall be and what shall not be through our efforts? No. And having a messiah complex that makes us think we can only makes matters worse. But worse too is the divorce of believing hopefully from acting hopefully. Isaiah 65 says of God, "I am about to create new heavens and a new earth." To say it is up to us to bring in the new creation is the sin of pride, even if it be under the banner of social justice. To say it is up to God alone, apart from us, to bring in the new creation is the sin of sloth, even if it parades under the banner of orthodoxy. God seeks neither the self-deluded nor the self-denying. God seeks those willing to believe the "no more" of Isaiah's vision—and to publicly enact that belief as we are able. And when we are not able, it is to trust that God has a stake in the restoration of justice. It is a stake that goes back all the way to the stories of our beginnings, beginnings given broad hints in Isaiah through the vocabulary and imagery of creation.

Back to the Future

No fewer than three times in Isaiah 65:17-18 does the verb "create" appear. It is the same word used to describe human creation in Genesis 1:27. It is the same word used to summarize the totality of God's creation in Genesis 2:3. Heavens and earth belong to the very first verse of Genesis, prefacing the order of days and works that will follow. Isaiah understands that for God's work of "no more" to be set in place, the undoing of an unfairness that has taken hold in creation involves a new start, a restoration of justice intended from the outset.

The analogy is far from perfect, but this restoration is akin to a function of the computer systems many of us use. Understand, please, my knowledge of computers is far more utilitarian (I can use them) than theoretical (I can't explain them). So forgive any technical errors I make in offering this comparison. Several months ago I found I had a problem with my operating system as a whole. Changes had been made that I didn't really want to maintain. And then I discovered this wonderful tool (software? utility?) called "system restore." It told me I could select a date in the past, and (in ways and with limitations I do not pretend to grasp) I could restore my system to the way it was on that date. And the system restore worked. Friends tell me that when really bad stuff happens, the needed fix is to reboot the system from scratch in order to start over again from the beginning.

"System restore" is suggestive of the way Isaiah 65 witnesses to the restoration of life's justice and "no more" to its unfairness. The language of Genesis is employed, for Genesis speaks the stories of our beginnings. The past will finally be released ("the former things shall not be remembered or come to mind"). The future will no longer be oppressed by the emptiness ("vain") or the inexplicably unjust sufferings ("calamity") that weigh existence down and lead us to think life's unfairness is perpetual. Such is our hope.

At this point it sounds as though we have tipped the scale fully in favor of Isaiah 65's being purely a scenario of a time yet to be, of a time that cannot be on this side of history or the grave. For surely the restoration—or reversal—as Isaiah speaks of it goes beyond the bounds of what is possible in this day and age. After all, look at verse 25. Wolves and lambs feeding together, lions eating straw like oxen; that's not how it is. Wolves don't feed *with* lambs but *on* them. Lions don't eat like oxen; they kill and devour them. Didn't Isaiah offer these very promises back in chapter 11 (verses 6-7)?

Well, yes and no. The lines about wolves and lambs and lions and oxen closely resemble that earlier oracle. The closing segment about no one hurting or destroying on God's holy mountain is practically verbatim in both chapters. But in between comes a significant difference. Once again a word and theme take us back into the creation narrative. In Isaiah 11, a nursing child is said to play on the hole of the asp. In Isaiah 65, however, the image differs strikingly: "the serpent— its food shall be dust!" In Genesis the serpent had served as the instrument of temptation. The serpent in Isaiah 65 retains the curse levied on it in the story of Genesis 3. As Walter Brueggemann suggests in his commentary on Isaiah 65: "The comment on the snake suggests that the divine oracle speaks about life in the real world and not in a never-never land."[1]

The work of *new* creation unfolds in *this* creation by God's hand and by the human hands, backs, and voices God employs. Is it within our power to make wolves and lions vegetarians? I think not. But it is within our power to choose another way of exercising power in this world that does not feed off the poor and vulnerable. It is within our power to choose other ways of settling disputes that do not inflict hurt and destruction on our enemies, on innocents hidden under the euphemism of "collateral damage," and on the earth itself. Some perceive hope as hard to accept because of its otherwordliness. In truth, hope is hard work invigorated by the promise of new heavens and earth and a willingness to set "no more" into the word and deed of witness in this world. Justice will be restored. That is the promise of faith. The real question is: will we be among those who walk the talk of hope, restoring justice where and when we are able?

Restoring Justice—And the Longing for Home

Isaiah introduces God's promise of new creation and justice restoration in these words: "I am about to . . . " These words can be a shoal on which we run aground or an impetus that gives fresh energy. The difference has to do with how we hear them in relationship to what we call "home." To those for whom home is and must always be immediate, identifiable with what we have known or have now, "I am about to" may tantalize with the prospect that this era is the one. More than a few have baptized a particular year with the time of God's restoration. Generally it has been a time in which they happened to live (who wants to predict a party they might not be part of?). When that time passes and the realm has not come, Christ has not returned, and justice has not been restored: bitterness can seize the day.

Another sense of "I am about to" implies that today always holds more promise than can possibly be fulfilled in its limited hours. Just around the corner, over the hill, and out of sight, there is some thing and some One so compelling as to make all the effort worthwhile. The gift of God's presence and companionship is ours already. In Jesus Christ, God has walked the path of "not yet" fully and deeply, even in the experience of death. Through the Holy Spirit, God continues to walk this path with us. Our view of all this may be, as Paul once wrote, through a mirror dimly—but not always. Sometimes, when we understand that the journey with the Spirit is the home we know now while on the way to a more intimate dwelling with God, we catch glimpses. And we live out in our lives the vision of what God intends to be.

We act justly. We say "no more" to the unfairness around, and sometimes within, us. In those moments we experience the promised restoration—in part but in truth. Those actions may come with great consequence, as for Telemachus or Rosa Parks. Or they may come in ways that seldom capture anyone's notice, save God's, who uses them in the wider work of restoration. As my colleague Roddy Hamilton spoke of hope's "sighting" in this world:

God lives within the process of changing our world. . . . Thus, small events and acts that bring life. It doesn't have to be Berlin Walls coming down, but children collecting money for something, people learning about crop rotation and farming skills in Africa, people marching for MAKEPOVERTYHISTORY, people buying goats and donkeys and toilets for Africa as Christmas presents to their family and friends.

When we act as we are able, when we act as we hope, justice finds home and restoration.

But the restoration for justice cries out for other rightings that surpass our ability. Who will restore justice for generations of abject poor who have known nothing but suffering until death? Who will restore justice for infants who have taken but a few breaths or elders who have had personality and spirit stolen from their final years? Who will restore justice to those innocents whom terror and oppression have silenced? Who will restore justice for a child playing in the field with her horse one moment and no more the next? For those, we wait upon the doing of justice by the One who calls us to do justice. For this is our hope.

I am about to create new heavens and a new earth. . . .

No more shall the sound of weeping be heard.

They shall not labor in vain or bear children for calamity.

So help us, God!

Chapter 5

HOPE
ORIENTING TO
GOD'S BLESSING

Matthew 5:3-12; Luke 6:20-21, 24-26

God is in the slums, in the cardboard boxes
where the poor play house. . . .
God is in the cries heard under the rubble of war.
God is in the debris of wasted opportunity and lives,
and God is with us if we are with them.
—BONO, *National Prayer Breakfast, February 2, 2006*

Judy and I wound around the back of a ridge, following a logging road until we came out on a landing left from an old logging operation. It overlooked the direction we had originally set out from. Looking down, we caught a glimpse of the road directly below us. The hike up the ridge had been steep, curved, and switchbacked. Surely a straight line down would be the quicker way out, rather than winding our way back the way we had come. We headed down.

Forty-five minutes later we were deep in a tangled thicket. Our ridge vantage point had not made visible the cuts and ravines that crisscrossed the way down. Going downhill was not the easy solution it seemed, as downhills quickly reversed into steep uphill banks careening off to one side or another. We lost our sense of direction. Afternoon was becoming evening. We decided we had to find a way back up. We did and caught another glimpse of the road. But rather than plunging down in that general direction, we selected a large snag (dead tree) that stood partway down. So oriented, we started again.

Even though the brush remained thick, we kept that snag in sight. Reaching its base, we could clearly see the road and a way out. One last scramble down, and we were safe.

Orienting. In Judy's and my case a visible landmark provided the way to locate ourselves in relationship to the way we needed to go. Orientation can be tricky because our understanding of where we are may be skewed. It can be like that on hikes. It can be like that on spiritual journeys. We bring assumptions of where we are and where God is. But assumptions and appearances can be grossly misleading. We need reliable points of orientation for our faith journeys. The teachings of Jesus, known as the Beatitudes, orient us to paths that are blessed of God—and others that are not.

Blessed or Happy

The Declaration of Independence of the United States asserts that God endows us with "certain unalienable Rights, that among these are Life, Liberty and the pursuit of Happiness." That latter right, the pursuit of happiness, touches in an odd way on Jesus' Beatitudes. Several translations and paraphrases of the Bible, such as the Good News Translation and the Living Bible, render "blessed" as "happy" in their versions of Matthew 5 and Luke 6. "Happy are those who are . . ." may sound like instructions for what will bring happiness in life. But is Jesus really laying out the program for a Christian pursuit of happiness? No.

The aim of the Beatitudes, not to mention the goal of spiritual growth, is not unhappiness. Sour expressions and dour outlooks are no more marks of maturity in faith than they are of healthy psyches. Hope that frowns is a contradiction. But unhappiness, by its very nature, is unappealing, unlikely to seduce us from a journey repeatedly identified in scripture with joy. Illusionary experiences of satisfaction or pleasure, which we may confuse with joy, are far more likely to deflect us from faith's path.

We live in an age that encourages such confusion. Consider our culture's depiction of happiness as "carefree" and "affluent." A "happy" scene would not include anyone or anything that might make us feel bad. Judy and I recently enjoyed visiting friends in Hawaii, our first trip there. The business district in the town where we stayed was busy with trade and nightlife. The region surrounding the town had its share of fabulous homes and condominiums, whose prices would make Seattle or Vancouver housing costs seem reasonable. But only a block or two away from the main commercial street in town were shacks. Tourists were not directed to those streets. Why spoil a good time? Why let those scenes get in the way of the pleasure of escape?

Happiness that relies on a state of mind in denial or avoidance of present reality is not happiness. Transitory amusement certainly is not what God bestows on those whom Jesus declares to be blessed in the Beatitudes of Matthew and Luke. To be blessed of God is not to know pleasure while remaining oblivious to hardships or injustice around us. To be blessed of God is to know God's favor and advocacy in the midst of situations that appear on the surface to be antithetical to what often passes for happiness among us.

Consider, for example, the very ones whom both Gospels identify in Jesus' Beatitudes as blessed of God: the poor, the hungry, those who weep, the persecuted. Jesus does not say that God blesses folks *with* poverty or hunger or tears or threat. No, the blessing—the assertion of God's favor—comes to those who are caught in such situations. The versions of these Beatitudes in Matthew and Luke differ somewhat. Some say that Matthew "spiritualizes" a more original teaching that Luke records. I would argue it is a case of both/and rather than either/or. God's blessing of poor and poor in spirit are equally stunning in a world that tramples not only on the impoverished but on those for whom blowing your own horn is not second nature. God's blessing of those who hunger for food or for justice runs counter to attitudes and institutions that treat the lack of food and justice as inevitable in this world and thus acceptable.

Poverty and hunger, grief and persecution are nothing to be happy about. Jesus' words of blessing on those who endure such circumstances is not to impose false-front smiles on faces but to infuse hope into lives. It is the hope that God does not rely on outward circumstances to reveal who is blessed and who is not. It is the hope that God holds those who traverse such difficult terrain in special favor. It is hope intended to spur those of us who claim the mantle of discipleship to go and be a source of blessing to those folks—and to trust in God's favor when we are numbered among them.

God's (Dis)Orienting Hope

In an old *Seinfeld* episode, George decides to act contrarian. He reasons that since his life has gone so poorly in so many ways, why follow the same decision-making instincts he has in the past? Why not do the exact opposite of what he normally would have done when choices present themselves? He puts the tactic in motion. "Opposite George" works.

That strategy is not unheard of in real life. Sometimes to turn and make a fresh start, we have to move in a direction opposite that of the past. Anyone who has struggled with addictive behavior will know something of this. You can't have one drink or toke like you always used to. You can't afford to run around with the same crowd that continues in the same self-destructive mode. Breaks have to be made. New directions have to be taken.

The biblical path of spiritual growth summons such movement on everyone's part. In traditional theological language, this is the movement of repentance. The Hebrew word for repentance, *shub*, means "to turn around." Its Greek counterpart, *metanoia*, is a compound word that combines the words for "change" and "mind." Repentance sets aside not only old ways of thinking but the actions associated with those thoughts and attitudes. It involves turning away from the old and turning toward the new. Where is hope in repentance? It resides in the possibility of change. We are not locked forever into former ways that have proved themselves inadequate. Hope offers the promise that new ways can be taken. Hope assures that even the discomfort brought by change is worth the renewal that can come.

Repentance has long been associated almost exclusively with sin and, more often than not, with sin narrowly defined as personal transgression and individual moral failure. We hear this view reflected in Ezekiel 18. There, the prophet teaches individual accountability as opposed to being judged on account of another: "It is only the person who sins that shall die" (18:4). John the Baptizer in the New Testament invites preparation for God's Messiah by "proclaiming a baptism of repentance for the forgiveness of sins" (Luke 3:3). Mark includes among Jesus' first words in his Gospel: "'Repent, and believe in the good news'" (1:15). Repentance of sin is clearly one landmark intended to orient us in new directions toward God.

But as the Baptizer and Jesus make surprisingly clear, that orientation may not point in either predictable or overtly "religious" directions. John does not orient seekers to the new life merely through a ritual washing. His proclamation of repentance becomes a disorienting word that encourages ordinary folk to share, not grasp, what little they may have. He advises soldiers and tax collectors to refrain from common practices that allow them to profit from their vocations (Luke 3:11-14). Later a young man who, for all practical purposes, is a paragon of piety approaches Jesus. The young man confesses he has kept all of the commandments from his youth. Nothing in the story indicates that Jesus does not take his assertion at face value. Indeed, Mark goes so far as to say that Jesus looks on him with love. Sin does not seem to be the concern here for repentance. Even so, Jesus' love requires turning. "'You lack one thing; go, sell what you own, and give the money to the poor, and you will have treasure in heaven; then come, follow me'" (Mark 10:21). The call to repentance when offered in love always invites rather than coerces. The young man chooses to walk away, grieving. One might say the young man walks away disoriented. Perfectly understandable and prior orienting presumptions about what makes for spiritual intimacy fall away. Jesus seeks change, even among the pious and the righteous. Why? Spiritual experience is not reducible to religious practices or formulas however revered. Spiritual experience comes in radical trust of God.

All of which leads us back to these Beatitudes of Jesus in Matthew and Luke. In Matthew the Beatitudes open that wider body of teaching known as the Sermon on the Mount; in Luke the sermon is on a plain. Many have interpreted the Sermon on the Mount as a manifesto of life lived in response to God's coming sovereign realm. As Moses brought Torah down from Sinai to order Israel's life, so from the "mount" Jesus delivers an ordering of life for this newly instructed community of God's people. Later in the sermon, he relays an extended series of "you have heard that it was said to those of ancient times. . . . But I say to you" teachings. In a sense, the Beatitudes have already employed that tactic. Instead of presenting an alternative to some specifics of existing law, however, the Beatitudes offer alternatives to outlooks prevalent in culture—then and now. To orient the community to God's new realm requires disorientation from commonly held yardsticks of spiritual well-being.

The Beatitudes are truly disorienting affirmations, whose acceptance relies on extraordinary trust. Consider how they would redirect the landmarks by which we locate ourselves and others in relationship to God. Conventional wisdom would say if you are poor, hungry, sorrowing, or wronged, then your life is not blessed. In less charitable moments it might even say you are cursed. *That wouldn't have happened to you if . . . ; you wouldn't be in that position if you worked harder or prayed with more faith. . . ; you've got to go along to get along. . .*

To all those judgments and attitudes, whether rendered on self or others, Jesus' Beatitudes disorient conventional wisdom with God's unconventional ways. This is especially true in that often-ignored corollary of the Beatitudes: the woes in Luke 6:24-26. The connection between those two sections is not just that the woes follow the blessings of the previous verses. They are intentionally paired as opposites: poor and rich, hungry and full, weeping and laughing, hated and spoken well of. On the surface who would not rather be in the position of those opposites: the well-off, the well-fed, the well-spirited, the well-liked? In fact, it would seem that the ones who enjoy those conditions in life would be the ones who are blessed of God with abundance and ease. Yet this is where the disorientation of repentance becomes critical: to free us from unfounded presumptions of what points to well-being with God.

Equally important, the Beatitudes orient us to the ones truly blessed of God. Jesus' Beatitudes say to the poor, the hungering, the mourning, the pursued: you are blessed. You are blessed of God. The Beatitudes orient us and all to the promise that present circumstances will not always be as they are now. For some that will come as warning, but for others it speaks great promise. The Beatitudes remind us that we cannot go on appearances alone to prove or disprove God's favor. Our hope resides, not in how things seem or appear at this moment in our lives or those of others but in the steady word of God's grace and advocacy. So Jesus' blessings orient and disorient us. They do so in hope of redirecting how we live in this present moment entrusted to us by God, in light of the future promised by God.

Now and Then

Scholars have observed that many slave owners in pre-Civil War America encouraged Christianity among their slaves, the rationale being that selected Bible passages would "proof-text" the present state of affairs. Ephesians 6:5 ("Slaves, obey your earthly masters") served such purposes. The encouragement of slaves to worship with whites, and efforts to limit religious instruction only to that provided by white instructors, sought to ensure that selectivity. That way, texts like Galatians 3:28 could be avoided ("there is no longer slave or free, . . . for all of you are one in Christ Jesus"). Another part of the slave owners' rationale had to do with translating biblical hope exclusively into notions of the hereafter. Limiting hope to a place and time yet to be offered less motive for seeking to transform the world as it was. Such hope would strip *now* from its outlook and concern. It would be pie in the sky in the sweet bye and bye.

Hope revealed in the Beatitudes is deeply rooted in *now*. Jesus does not say, "Blessed *will be*. . ." Each and every beatitude begins with the words: "blessed *are* . . ." As if to underscore the point, two of the Beatitudes in Luke add *now* to their declaration of God's favor ('"Blessed are you who are hungry now, . . . who weep now'"). That emphasis on the present, on God's blessing in this moment, serves two purposes. First, it affirms God's favor for folk who live in conditions and circumstances that might otherwise strip *now* of its meaning and worth. It reminds those caught in such times that neither life nor God's grace is put on hold until those times pass. In experiences that devalue people, Jesus says your life is valued and blessed by God. In spite of this experience, there is cause to hope.

Second, in affirming such favor and value, the emphasis on the present in Jesus' Beatitudes urges us to treat such folk now as God's blessed ones, not God's discards. We do hope that God's coming reign will restore justice, but that does not excuse the church for not bringing the gifts and qualities of God's commonwealth to bear now on those who are burdened in the present. The Beatitudes identify the persons for whom Jesus' followers are to channel God's blessing. In a similar fashion the Beatitudes identify those with whom Christian community is to be entered today. All of Luke's Beatitudes are offered in second-person address ('"Blessed are you . . . '"). Jesus speaks to the poor and mourning, the hungry and persecuted of his day. He bids them welcome into community with the empowering word that they are blessed of God. How do we offer that affirmation and invitation?

The Beatitudes are about *now*, but they are also about *then*. With few exceptions, the Beatitudes link the present experience of God's blessing ("Blessed are . . . ") with a futured promise ("for they/you will . . . "). Consider for a moment the promises offered: comfort, inheritance of the earth, filling, mercy, sight of God, naming as children of God, laughter. In some ways we do not wait for God's realm fully established to experience such gifts. We can know and give comfort now. We can enjoy and share the gifts of earth. We can be filled and receive mercy, see God and be called God's child and find joy now.

But in truth, the full measure of those promises eludes us in this present age. Try as we might, we never completely find comfort when a loved one dies. Try as we might, our experience of the earth as that blue marble spinning in space without sight of fence or conflict or pollution escapes us. We do catch glimpses of God in sacrament and in faces, but much remains mystery. We may want to know ourselves and others as God's children; but history, bias, and experience keep bringing up other names and labels to cloak that core identity. Those who would load everything into this life, all hopes and aspirations, all beauty and all possibility, even for the best of reasons, stumble.

Sometimes the stumbling comes because of the temptations' allure as represented in Luke's listing of woes. Goods separated from sharing. Laughter divorced from empathy. Popularity at the cost of ethics. Sometimes the stumbling comes universally. Like Ebenezer Scrooge under the influence of the spirit of Christmas future, we come upon a gravestone and realize it is our own. Death will come to all. And in Paul's eloquent insight, "If for this life only we have hoped in Christ, we are of all people most to be pitied" (1 Cor. 15:19).

As Christ's disciples we cannot hope apart from the future, and we cannot live detached from the present. Jesus' Beatitudes straddle present and future, now and then, for the sake of vocation and promise. The present orients us to the time in which the words of blessedness aim to affect the conduct of our lives. The future orients us to purposes and promises that may be fleeting or clouded in these moments. There is more to be known and hoped than what is now. By providing such orientation to present blessing and future promise, the Beatitudes help us find the way through this life with direction, integrity, and hope.

Orienting to God's Blessing—and the Longing for Home

In 1973 the American evangelical lawyer William Stringfellow wrote a book titled *An Ethic for Christians and Other Aliens in a Strange Land*. In it he sought to understand the times and nation in which he lived through biblical lenses—specifically, through the book of Revelation. His choice of title revealed his perspective that to live with biblically driven ethics in such a context was to be out of sync with the norms of modern-day values and powers.

As much as things change, some things remain the same. In spite of the perils of copyright law, Stringfellow's title would be a perfect title for a work on Jesus' Beatitudes. For once we get past cozy feelings born of familiarity with these words, we may find how they too are out of sync with norms of modern-day values and powers. The Beatitudes are not at home with what the world at large sees as blessed, whether by God or anyone else. To perceive the Beatitudes as orienting us in a homeward direction requires no small amount of faith. We are not accustomed to see the poor get much of anything, except poorer. The last time I watched the news, those who busy themselves inheriting the earth or ruining it by acting as if they do have rights of ownership seem anything but meek. As for the peacemakers—well, we have all sorts of other names to call those people. Yet Jesus calls all these and more blessed.

Jesus' blessing of such ones and the homeward direction toward which those blessings orient us catches us off guard. It runs counter to what we usually hear said and blessed among us, which is the point. The Beatitudes remind those who would be Christ's disciples that home for us is something other than "business as usual." In response to a question about what causes you to have hope in a world frequented by unhopeful events, my friend Jan Seale offered this:

> The unhopeful events are the "racket" of the world, that is, the noisy perhaps catastrophic nature events and the human bumbling and silliness of war. The hopeful events are often quieter: a forest regrowing after a fire, a person recovering to a useful life after having her heart redesigned, the five sun-breasted Great Kiskadee flycatchers perched in my backyard calling and singing to one another. God has trusted us to know and recognize the signs of hope, but they are often quiescent, in their own spiritual sphere, the coincidental, the "against all odds," the powerful calling of the Spirit at odd times.

The Beatitudes sound this "against all odds" witness with their quiet but firm assertion of the ones and the ways blessed of God. "Blessed are . . . " They invite us to orient our lives to these landmarks of God's blessings. They do not promise that we will never end up in tights spots or tangled thickets again, but we are graced through them with sight of where and for whom God's favor may be found:

This present moment and its possibilities for change and renewal
will not be lost;
the futured promise and its hope for what will yet be
will not be lost;
for the word of God's blessing will endure and
come to fruition;
As will the ones whom God blesses.
Now and for all time.

Chapter 6

HOPE
FINDING OURSELVES LOVED

Luke 15:1-3, 11-32

---

*I equate the phrase "longing for home" with a longing for a deep
intimacy with God. God is my true home. At the moment
there is a sense of disconnectedness, a separation, a kind of
prodigal experience. Yet I believe that even though I am a long
way off, God has seen me and is running to meet me.*
—SHARON HARDING

I magine this parable transported into a contemporary church setting.
If Jesus' listeners had been a United Church of Christ or Presbyterian
congregation, the Committee on Ministry would be dispatching a
mediator. If they had been a Lutheran or United Methodist congregation, the bishop would be naming a conflict-resolution team staffed
by the bishop's assistant or district superintendent to defuse the explo-
sive situation. For the center aisle in this imagined congregation facing Jesus divided more than pews. On one side tax collectors and
sinners sprawled about, many having gotten but a few hours of sleep
after partying until the wee hours. On the other side Pharisees and
scribes sat rigid, clothes freshly pressed and minds neatly set. One
side snickered at the hypocrites across the aisle. The other side shook
heads in disgust at the sort of folks the church lets in these days. Both
sides likely wondered about what kind of leader would put up with
those people. And perhaps, in thoughts that rarely saw the light of day,
a few may have even wondered about what kind of leader would welcome the likes of *me.* Jesus faced a dilemma. Would he lambaste the

sinners? Would he put the self-righteous in their place? Or would he tell a story about what it means to be family in the family of God?

To find others loved by God, others with whom we disagree and whose presence for many reasons offends us, can be demanding. That demanding nature may only be rivaled by the scandal of considering ourselves as loved by God. For who knows better than we do the failures that have littered our past and tangled our present? Who knows better than we do the baggage we have carried so long until its presence offers us bizarre comfort? That sense of disconnectedness and separation that Sharon identified in the opening quote haunts more than a few. That haunting can block our path to God. How can we hope to find ourselves, much less others, loved by God? The homeward journey unfolds in Jesus' story of dysfunctional children and a prodigal parent.

A House Divided . . . and Divided . . . and Divided

In biology, cellular division is not only a fact of life, it is the means of life. Worn-out cells are replaced by newly produced cells. Complex organisms, including humans, could not exist if cells could not divide. Division means hope. But there is a name for cells that divide indefinitely unchecked, without cease or regard for the organism's health: the name is cancer.

A cancer is at work in the divisions that run amok in Jesus' parable. There is the division of younger from family. This initial movement seems innocent enough. The need to find self apart from family definitions is universal and necessary. Sad are the cases of adults whose identities never grow beyond childhood dependencies or decisions made for them by others. The problem within the parable, however, is the nature of this first division. "'Give me the share of property that will belong to me'" is only slightly more polite than declaring: *You have not died soon enough, so I'll take what's due me now.* The ensuing division of property window-dresses the skewering of relationship by lack of care and respect.

There follows the subsequent division of the younger from himself. If that sounds odd, listen again to this line of the story: "when he came to himself." To come to oneself presumes that part of this child had gone somewhere else. To identify that "somewhere" as the foreign land or dissolute living or the swine pens only scratches the surface. All of those places and activities represent a separation of this youth from his life's moorings and his true self. Finally the story evidences the division between elder and younger siblings. The younger remains unaware of this division, for the parent bears the brunt of it. Each of these divisions careens out of control, threatening the viability of this organism named family with death in relationship.

Cancerous divisions also run rampant among the audience Jesus addresses. The scene imagined at the beginning of this chapter provides one portrayal of those divisions. Pharisees and scribes provide easy targets. Does not Jesus frequently join in the chorus against legalistic nitpicking that keeps the letter of the law but fails its spirit? Does not Jesus time and again show the hypocrisy of slavish interpretations of sabbath law that effectively squelch responses to human need? "Religious hypocrisy" is a charge that rolls off our tongues with relative ease when rebuking the divisions it can, has, and does engender.

But let us not deceive ourselves into thinking that divisions arise only because of the pride-blinded foibles of these guardians of morality. I for one would be utterly amazed if the tax collectors and sinners did not set themselves apart. I hear them dividing the world into realists like themselves from head-in-the-clouds pietists. I hear them asserting that if you're going to sin, you might as well do it up good as opposed to uptight hypocrites who think it but never do it. I have heard (and sometimes said) such things myself. Such divisions split these groups in Jesus' day and our own, threatening the viability of any community that would attempt to hold them together.

A cancer is at work in the body of Christ when divisions, even in Jesus' name, wreak havoc in community. Like the parable's characters, like its initial audience, we too seem disposed to dividing ourselves this way and that. Younger and elder, tax collectors and Pharisees:

ancient names for modern fracture lines. Progressives versus evangeli-cals. Denominational versus nondenominational. The possibilities stretch endlessly before us as do the separations among us. In the right —or wrong—circumstances, we may even find our energies drained by the toll such divisions exact upon purveyors and victims alike.

In Jesus' parable, what will become of family in the midst of its fracturing divisions? What can possibly heal two irreconcilable posi-tions as posed by the younger's request and the elder's resentment? At stake in the audience to whom Jesus tells this parable is what will become of community in the midst of its fracturing divisions. What can possibly heal two vastly differing groups as those who serve as moral compasses in this world and those whose morals have no sense of direction? At stake in the church whom Jesus gathers now is what will become of community in the midst of our fracturing divisions. What can possibly heal the chasms between advocates and adver-saries of gay rights or proponents and opponents of a woman's right to choose abortion or any number of lines drawn in the sand where those who are not for us must therefore be considered against us . . . and against God?

There is a name for cells that divide indefinitely unchecked without cease or regard for the organism's health: the name is cancer. Those words from the opening paragraph of this section notwithstanding, I would not naively say that any and all divisions in the body of Christ are cancer-ous. Some divisions promote new life. In the most onerous of situa-tions, division may keep alive some truth or community that would not otherwise survive. But even so, the church's witness to one Lord, one faith, one baptism is sorely tested by the epithets we throw at one another for the sake of "our side." The service of Christ is splintered when our energies are absorbed by cataloguing the sins of others while ignoring our own. In the end, neither the children in the para-ble nor its opposed audience members nor you or I get to decide who's in and who's out, who's family and who's not. That task—and our hope—falls to the character and storyteller who risks love.

The Danger and Grace of Love

Writing in *An American Childhood*, Annie Dillard reminisces about her childhood. More than once in that work, she remarks in wonder at the risk parents (including her own) take in allowing their children to be taught Bible stories.

> The adult members of society adverted to the Bible unreasonably often. What arcana! Why did they spread this scandalous document before our eyes? If they had read it, I thought, they would have hid it. They didn't recognize the vivid danger that we would, through repeated exposure, catch a case of its wild opposition to their world.[1]

Nostalgia and familiarity aside, I would rate this particular parable of Jesus high in that danger zone. Surely it earns at least a PG-13 rating, if not an R (requires an accompanying adult or guardian). Why? It flagrantly and willfully exercises love that jeopardizes all.

To be sure, love as demonstrated in this parable serves the prodigals among us just fine. But consider the elder: the stay-at-home, the responsible one, the one who caused no trouble all these years, the one who was a son rather than a disappointment to his father. Think of what love probably looks like to the elder child. Caving in. Making a spectacle of yourself in front of the neighbors, in front of me. Love takes shape in the reckless embrace of the errant younger and the careless throwing of a party for one who gutted the family once already, emotionally and financially. Love takes shape in what must seem like amnesia to the elder child.

Do we see no danger in that? Such love may be well and good for prodigals, but it scares respectable folk who order lives, families, businesses, and churches on the importance of consequences and duty: that is, folk like us. Can we imagine the damage done to families and communities if love's reckless embrace of prodigals became the norm? Who would be left to do the work? What would motivate us?

I believe the elder clearly sees the danger of such love. But he at least is in a position to stand to the side, to stay out in the field, to steer clear of the returning prodigal. He can avoid for the time being the choice to love or not.

The father in the parable cannot. For this parent, love is even more dangerous because it requires immediate and consequential decisions on his part. Some might argue the loving thing to have done at the outset would have been to deny the younger his inheritance: "I will not give it up to you. I'm not dead yet, you know. You've got a lot to learn, and you're going to stay here and learn it!" This parent, however, exhibits the sort of love that understands freedom as both reward and punishment. This hard and dangerous love comprehends that letting go may provide the only path for a wanderer to find home or discover hope. The danger comes in knowing that letting go does not guarantee return.

Later this father cannot avoid the choice to love or not when a bedraggled child-who-chose-to-be-a-stranger comes walking into view. The choices are legion. Turn your back, lock the gate, bar the door, shut him out as he shut you out. Or keep your distance, fold your arms, listen to what he has to say, watch him grovel, make him pay the way he made you pay in the currency of heartbreak. Or start to move, break into run, throw your arms around him before he has a chance to speak.

Which choice would you make? Or maybe even more pertinent, what choice have you made? When faced with one whose presence disappointed if not hurt you, whose absence made you revisit all those aches and voids, what did you do then? Operate on the basis of "fool me once, shame on you; fool me twice, shame on me"? Set up conditions for reentry, proofs this will not happen again? Or break down and cry and laugh at the craziness of life restored just for the love of it? Deep in our hearts, we know the love practiced by this father is dangerous and seditious. But even now one more choice remains, since one more son remains.

In the end the father cannot avoid the choice to love or not in the face of his elder child's justified resentment. The elder child throws "this son of yours" in the father's face. The breaking of family ties involves not only the absurdity of the younger one's behavior but, for the elder child, arises from the old man's pandering acceptance. In the elder's sight "this son of yours" carries a stinging rebuke not only of a brother no longer a brother but a father no longer a father. Defiance seems a stock and trade of this brood of children at finish as well as start. But this parent does not relent. Luke has him address the irate and aggrieved elder with a word that literally means "child." "Child" does not express ownership or rebuke. It is a word of endearment, a statement of relationship. This expression of love embraces the one who thought love had to be earned, even as it earlier embraced one who knew it couldn't be. Such love is dangerous, because it declines to play favorites. Love doesn't wait on proper confessions or resentments set aside. Love simply, yet profoundly, finds us before we find ourselves—regardless of what we think of God's choice of company.

That last point turns the parable from wrestling with love's dangers to opening to its grace. Many parables are about grace. What makes this parable unique in its telling of grace is its setting. Relationships in the close quarters of family pose remarkable possibility. Where else can grace be so tested? They are the ones for whom love is a given at birth, who subsequently can make us wonder if loving strangers might be the easy way out. If grace can be possible here, holding both prodigal and dutiful, is there hope for us?

So Jesus Told *Them* This Parable

Technically speaking, Luke penned those words to introduce the parable of the lost sheep and the lost coin, two parables that precede the prodigal son and loving father. But stylistically speaking, Luke's words hold true as introduction for this parable as well. It is said Jesus told it to *them*. And who is the audience? Actually, the question is who *are* the audiences? Plural.

There is, first of all, the audience Jesus addressed according to the text. It is a mixed and divided group: tax collectors and sinners, Pharisees and scribes. Some commentators narrow the focus to one or the other. "Them" gets understood either as tax collectors and sinners (*aren't you grateful God welcomes the likes of you?*) or Pharisees and scribes (*don't you get it about God's grace?*). However, Jesus, being a good preacher, would not single some out and ignore others. The parable offers a cutting edge for both groups. So Jesus' telling *them* this parable seems a statement of inclusion. Everybody got a word that day. Whether that word got heard as judgment or grace, warning or hope depended, as it always does, less on the speaker and more on the listener.

Jesus addressed a second audience with this parable. More properly stated, Luke addressed a second audience through Jesus' words: the audience of Luke's day, the community and church for whose sake these words were collected in this particular Gospel in its particular order with its particular themes. We get clues about this community from the choices Luke made in this Gospel's telling, in comparison and contrast with the other Gospels. Luke, for example, goes to great lengths to speak of the role of outsiders. Shepherds are the first celebrants of Christmas. Samaritans do good things. Women exercise faith at the Gospel's beginning ("'Let it be with me according to your word'") and serve as resurrection's first witnesses. The poor and the rich figure largely in Luke's Gospel. Mary sings in anticipation of God's filling the hungry and dismissing the rich empty-handed. Jesus tells the parable of Lazarus and the rich man and, in doing so, hints at the upheaval of status quos on earth and in the realm to come.

In other words, if Luke's collection can be trusted: Luke's audience is a community wrought with divisions, including economic and gender, insiders and outsiders (most likely Jewish Christians and Gentile Christians). Any one of those fracture lines could have broken Luke's community into pieces. Any one of those dividing lines could have insisted that only one side had hope, only one side had truth, only one side had love. But to men and women, Gentile and Jew, rich and poor, this Gospel in general and this parable in particular were told. Its telling reminded those on the outside looking in that prodigals are welcomed and loved and reminded those on the inside looking out that "'you are always with me, and all that is mine is yours.'" All will find themselves loved and be nudged toward mending divisions by practicing such love themselves.

There is still another audience to be considered: us. The biblical stories may be interesting for the light they shed on the characters in the narratives or the audience originally addressed, but "interesting" does not change lives or transform the status quo of our spirituality. To borrow from Annie Dillard's perspective, the stories are danger-ous—dangerous because they disrupt and infuse our lives with their wild opposition to the world as it is. And in doing so, these stories speak anew to us that they might live anew through us.

Jesus tells us of prodigals because we have our share of them wan-dering off among us and from us. They are prodigals who, in critical moments of coming to themselves, stand in need of a place that will welcome and not interrogate. Jesus tells us of resentful elders because we have our share of them populating positions of power and respon-sibility in community and in church. As with the prodigals, those eld-ers need a place that will assure them of love's gift even when they insist it must be earned. Jesus tells of a loving parent because, well, let us hope we have enough of these folks in our families and on our church councils and in our corridors of powers. These are the ones who understand love must be risked to overcome divisive splits. These are the ones whose love, like the love of God, allows for the freedom of others. The father in the parable had no certainties at the outset that the prodigal would ever return. In the end, Luke leaves the narrative wide open as to whether that elder will ever come in from the field and rejoin the family. The father does not drag him kicking and screaming against his will into community, into love, because that would be a contradiction. Love offers, love gives, love invites. And then, love waits. And hopes. . . . Do you?

Finding Ourselves Loved—and the Longing for Home

Of all the texts chosen for this book's consideration of hope and its longing for home, this parable makes the most obvious connection.

Everything about it has to do with home. A prodigal leaves, longs, and returns. An elder stays, endures, and resents. The one constant seems to be this parent, whose love is both the eye of the storm and, to some degree, the storm's cause.

Longing for home weaves into the lines and between the lines of this story. For the prodigal it was longing born of absence and regret. For the elder it may have been a longing for things as they were before the ne'er-do-well showed up again. Or maybe, just maybe, he longed to be so graciously loved rather than having to earn love. I would venture to say, we share both of those sets of longings within our souls. The truth telling of this parable comes not just in the welcome received by prodigals. It also tells the truth in the father's going out to meet the elder as he had earlier gone out to meet the younger. Finding ourselves loved is not a morality tale. Receiving God's love is not a matter of making ourselves better and proving ourselves dutiful. Those are all responses to love, but they are not love's cause. Finding ourselves loved involves a journey of coming to ourselves and recognizing that love—and home—have been there all along.

In that sense, hope as the longing for home is not always written in future tense. For those who internalize this parable's grace, hope as the longing for home comes in the realization we have that home, that place, in love already. But we do not have it all to ourselves. The parable insists to the elders among us: the family of God embraces the prodigals. "'This brother of yours was dead and has come to life.'" Surprisingly, and every bit as graciously, the parable insists to the prodigals among us that God's family embraces the elders. "'You are always with me.'" Division that has always plagued the community of God and vexes us still is *not* the final state of things. If only we had eyes to see and spirit to accept, it is not even the *current* state of things. God loves prodigal and elder alike now. That recognition forms the core of this parable. That is also its call: to live as the God-loved reconciled community in this day. In Jesus Christ we have found ourselves and those from whom we are estranged, loved.

In that love we find our place.
  In that place we find our hope.
    "You are always with me."
"'This brother of yours was dead and has come to life.'"
    So Jesus told this parable to them . . .
      so Jesus tells it to us.
        That we who have been lost, divided, may be found.

Chapter 7

HOPE

RESURRECTING LIFE

1 Corinthians 15:12-26, 55-58

The immortality of the soul is an opinion—
the resurrection of the dead is a hope.
The first is a trust in something immortal in the human being,
the second is a trust in the God who calls into being
the things that are not, and makes the dead live.

—JÜRGEN MOLTMANN

John Donne, famous English poet and clergyman of the early seventeenth century, may be best remembered for an essay that contains the phrases "for whom the bell tolls" and "no man is an island." But John Donne was also a husband whose wife died when she was only thirty-three. Among several works attributed to that trying experience, "Sonnet X" of his *Holy Sonnets* offers an especially powerful rendering of hope.

> Death, be not proud, though some have called thee
> Mighty and dreadful, for thou art not so.
> . . . .
> Thou art slave to fate, chance, kings, and desperate men,
> And dost with poison, war, and sickness dwell;
> And poppy or charms can make us sleep as well
> And better than thy stroke; why swellest thou then?
> One short sleep past, we wake eternally,
> And Death shall be no more: Death, thou shalt die!'

The death of death is what this chapter and its hope considers. The New Testament language for that is resurrection. It is language that occasionally has been confused with resuscitation. It is language that some in the church have used as a bludgeon to insist on narrow explanations rather than as an invitation to trust what remains mystery. It is language that has been short-circuited by philosophical excursions into the destiny and transmigration of disembodied souls. Part of this chapter's theme of "resurrecting life" will deal with what Christian hope does and does not pronounce by way of resurrection. Beyond that, it will invite us to dare to hope what Donne and the apostle Paul, and long before them Isaiah and Micah, announced: the death of death. The longing for a place and home beyond death's demise means neither escape from nor denial of death's present reality among us. Such longing means that we trust in a God who has set extraordinary things into motion in the raising of Jesus. God is even now in the midst and work of resurrecting life.

High Stakes

I admit it. Occasionally I have watched snippets of the current rage in sports television: high stakes poker games. Maybe my fascination comes from growing up along the Mississippi River, where stories of riverboat gamblers sipping mint juleps formed part of long-ago traditions of river life. With the rest of the audience watching these modern-day card table showdowns, I have a distinct advantage over the players. I get to see what cards everyone holds. The format sets me up to imagine what I would do if I held this or that hand. With those stacks of chips before me, what would I risk in hopes of the right turn of cards not yet seen? I find it hard to understand the amounts of money ventured during the betting. Rather ordinary looking people calmly push into the pot what amounts to the annual gross income of my wife and me—sometimes two or three times that amount. Would I do that, not knowing the turn of the cards? Sometimes players will go all in, betting everything they have. If they win, they take the hand

and sometimes the game. But if they lose, it will be the last hand they play. No second chance; all is lost.

Can you imagine putting everything on the line for a single outcome that will either secure you or undo you? Actually, I can. I can remember occasions where, in word if not in deed, I have done something similar. Sometimes the setting has been a sanctuary. Sometimes the setting has been the chapel of a funeral home. Many times the setting has been a cemetery. In all those times I have stood before a gathered people—some weeping, some carrying on stoically with a mix of emotions tumbling inside. Often times, between me and them, has stood a metal or wooden box that contains a lifeless body or an urn with ashes. Inside, a father, a mother, a child, a friend, a colleague, a neighbor. I have stood before those gathered people with service and sermon notes on a podium or in a notebook, laid out like so many cards on a table. I could see the hand that had been dealt to those folks who wondered if anything could bring comfort or peace in such a time as this. The hand had taken form in that casket or in the urn, and its power and grief could not be denied. But I pushed in all the chips I had that day as I uttered words like these:

> I am the resurrection and the life . . . fear not, for I am with you. . . .
> receive your child into the arms of your mercy, into the blessed rest of
> everlasting peace. . . . we commit this body or these ashes to the earth
> in confident and certain hope of the resurrection to eternal life. . . . If
> we have been united with Christ in a death like Christ's, we shall certainly be united with Christ in a resurrection like Christ's.

Resurrection sounds awe-fully strange in our world. It may flow easily off our tongues and through our minds when lilies bedeck sanctuaries and trumpet fanfares usher in Easter sunrise services. Then and there, we expect such words. But when we lower a loved one into a grave, resurrection catches in our throat. Where is it when we need it?

To speak of resurrection hope is, in the face of things as they are, a gamble and a risk. It has been awhile since we've had a resurrection around here. But to live the resurrection hope, well, that goes far beyond the gambit taken by presiding ministers at funeral or memorial services. To live the resurrection hope is to put all the chips on the table in the form of one's own life. Extreme examples of what it means to live that risk may be found in the martyrs of the church. People as ancient as Stephen and others more recent (Dietrich Bonhoeffer, Archbishop Oscar Romero) have put all on the line quite literally. Without the hope of resurrection, their actions and risks might be labeled as foolish or worse. For if life consists solely of the span between first breath and last, why do anything that would hasten the latter? It would make no sense. Its impact would be subject to the limits of human memory and the schemings of human tyranny.

Martyrs, however, are not the only ones who demonstrate the risk of resurrection hope. That risk is taken by any who live and choose, who love and serve in defiance of fear and death as having the final word. To define human existence exclusively within the boundaries between birth and death cedes the upper hand to those who will stop at nothing, including death, to have their way. It strips ethics of any horizon line of accountability beyond good-natured altruism at best, and "it's a dog-eat-dog world" at worst. Paul has it right when he counsels the community at Corinth: "If for this life only we have hoped in Christ, we are of all people most to be pitied." Why? Without resurrection, unconditional love is folly in the face of brute force and apathetic injustice. Without resurrection, we may live with the naive optimism that the world might get better, but we will be without hope that the world will ever be truly transformed. Without resurrection, death will always and everywhere hold the final word.

I have respected friends who firmly believe that death brings utter finality, and they peacefully accept their destiny in those terms. At death they will return to the earth and live on in the decomposition—more positively, composting—of their bodies into other life forms. They will continue to be part of the cosmos until the sun burns out and whatever comes next, if there is then such a thing as "next." I do not deny the science of what will become of our physical material. But the hope to which we are called in the raising of Jesus avows a different perspective. Resurrection asserts a decisive break in the cycle of life's ending in death because of the God who is able and graciously disposed to call into being the things (and ones) that are not. Resurrection invites trust that God will make us whole again, and death itself will be no more.

Death itself will be no more. Only such hope can make our witness to life and justice credible in the face of fear and death that otherwise hold the upper hand. Only such hope can make courage a viable expression of what the future holds rather than a noble but vain disregarding of an inevitable fate. Only such hope can push all of our chips on the table when life is at stake, not as an act of foolish desperation but as a trust of holy intent. For we are resurrectionists.

Opinions and Hopes

It might seem an odd thing that we have come this far into a chapter on resurrection without explaining how it happens or defining precisely what it is. The reason for that comes from the Gospels—more precisely, from the silence of the Gospels. Read Matthew 28. Read Mark 16. Read Luke 24. Read John 20–21. Neither the Gospel writers nor the risen Jesus teach the science of resurrection. The actual event itself has no witnesses. The closest we get is Matthew 28 when Mary Magdalene and the other Mary go to see the tomb. There is an earthquake, and an angel of God rolls back the stone. The guards "[become] like dead men." The women stand their ground but do not see Jesus emerge from the tomb. They hear the news of Easter from one identified as an angel; they receive a word that sends them on their way. Only then do they, like we, encounter the risen Jesus. From the outset, resurrection is known only in its results.

I take the Gospels' silence on the "facts" of resurrection to be a signal against reducing Easter faith to a formula about how it happened to Jesus and how it may or may not happen to us. Wounds still seen and meals still partaken suggest continuity with life as it is now. Confusion with a gardener and appearing among disciples in spite of locked doors suggests discontinuity with the way things are now. But how, and what, is resurrection exactly? The Gospels do not say, beyond their witness to an emptied tomb and appearances of the risen Jesus.

Paul does offer words about the "how and what" of resurrection (1 Cor. 15:35-54), but he speaks there far more in metaphor than definition. In the end, even Paul invokes the M word: *mystery* (verse 51). To venture beyond resurrection as mystery treads paths uncharted by the Bible's evangelical witness. And woe to those who think Christian faith requires us to line up behind this opinion on the exact nature of bodies reconstituted or that opinion on spirit over matter defining the person. Resurrection faith is not anchored in the details of "how" but in the affirmation of "who." God raised Jesus. Trust in God is the point. All sorts of opinions surround conjecture about resurrection. But in the end, opinions do not save or resurrect or give hope. God does.

Some people interpret the great variety of opinion about resurrection as indication that it cannot be true or real. I take it as a simple reflection of the human mind to attempt multiple explanations of that which remains, at its heart, mystery. A Latin phrase, *sui generis*, means "of its own kind." A *sui generis* is something unique, standing on its own. Creation is a *sui generis*. Consider all the ways in which the peoples of this world, its scientists, and its religionists have sought to explain or describe that elemental truth in which we live and move and have our being. All approach the same truth of creation's existence from differing angles. The approaches are so different and so multiple, you might think it impossible to finally and definitively speak of creation. You would be right. Scientifically, religiously, literally: creation remains mystery. But mystery does not mean it cannot be true. It is hard to argue against the truth of creation when you stand hip-deep in it.

So it is with resurrection. Our inability to explain it in any systematic, unified way does not mean it cannot be true. Now, my friends on the nonresurrection side of the equation would argue that neither does the inability to explain resurrection or baptize it as "mystery" prove it is true. And they would be right. But resurrection was not meant to be proved but trusted, to be followed as a peculiar way of hope in this world. The risen Jesus did not hand out essay tests for us to describe our opinions of resurrection. The risen Jesus bid disciples then and now to follow him on the way, even and especially when that way leads us toward or into the gates of death.

Taunts and Commissions

In modern athletics "talking trash" to opponents is commonplace on the court or the field. To be sure, some sports surround themselves with traditions of genteel respect that restrict attitudes and emotions to raised eyebrows. But when defensive and offensive linemen come to a set or rugby players scrum or point guards face off, talk does not turn to the genius of Mozart over against the virtues of Beethoven. It gets ugly. It gets personal. Some of us who have coached youth sports have sought to steer our charges away from that, to insist on skills and execution. But the truth of the matter is, taunting has deep roots in fields of competition. Those roots go much deeper and much farther back than playground learnings of "nyah, nyah, nyah, nyah, nyah."

In Lamentations 3:63 Jeremiah, in his experience of persecution, writes that he is the object of his enemies' taunt-songs. He pleads for remembrance by God, so that his taunters do not win the day. In 1 Samuel 17, Goliath taunts the Israelites, daring them to send out a man to face him in combat. When David finally steps out of the ranks to face him, the taunt continues, "'Am I a dog, that you come to me with sticks?'" Goliath, however, learns a hard truth about taunts. You can't just talk the game. In the end the Philistine falls victim to the one he thought he could demoralize or frighten with insults and arrogance. Taunts can be a weapon, but they are not much of a shield. You have to be able to back up the words . . . or to have someone who is capable of doing that for you.

Paul closes his chapter on resurrection in First Corinthians with what is, for all practical purposes, a taunt. "Where, O death, is your victory? Where, O death, is your sting?" It is the theological equivalent of wiggling your fingers underneath your chin while saying "neener,

neener, neener." It is an extraordinary word of defiance and faith. But it a very risky word.

Where is its risk? Consider the taunt of death's "victory." If we were simply keeping score, death would hold a seemingly insurmountable lead in this game. One population researcher has estimated that about 106 billion human beings have been born in the world's history. How many resurrections have there been? One. So with about 6.5 billion people alive today, that would roughly mean that 99,499,999,999 have not been resurrected. On the face of it, Paul raises up his taunt against death with the numbers definitely not in his favor and getting worse every passing second. If your team was losing by 99 billion runs, would you be talking trash to the opponent? It takes either astonishing faith or naïveté to mock death's victory.

But Paul's taunt goes further. "Where, O death, is your *sting?*" (italics added). Though the question seems rhetorical in the passage, it need not be. After all, what about the sting of death felt at the edge of that grave where we bury parent or child or companion or friend? Or what about the sting we experience when hearing the word *terminal* in our own diagnosis or finding ourselves permanently bedridden? Death brings the sting of leave-taking, of experiencing the truth of our mortality in deep ways not dismissed by mere words.

Some would defend the logic or safety of Paul's taunt by pointing out he defines *sting* here as "sin," not as the frailty of human emotion in the face of death. Even so, "where, O death, is your sting?" is a taunt whose outcome must still be taken on faith. After all, has Easter eradicated sin? We need only check out the news if we harbor any illusions about that. If the sting of death is nowhere to be seen, why do six million children under the age of five die each year from hunger (from Church World Service, "Facts Have Faces: Hunger in a World of Plenty")? Or in other words, why do we allow the equivalent of the 9/11 tragedy to happen five times a day, every day of the year?

Taunting death's victory and sting is, like most taunts, an assertion about a future whose outcome is still very much in doubt. Like most taunts, it relies on something (or someone) more than mere words to back up the claim. For Paul that something is resurrection and that someone is the God who raised Jesus. In the face of incredible odds, in the midst of overwhelming evidence to the contrary, Paul taunts that death's own death is on the way. It is in sight—that is, in the sight of faith. In Jesus' resurrection a door cracks open, and Paul catches a glimmer of light that is hope. From that glimmer he closes his meditation on resurrection not with another taunt—but with a commission to the community at Corinth and to us.

> "Therefore, my beloved, be steadfast, immovable, always excelling in the work of the Lord, because you know that in the Lord your labor is not in vain" (1 Cor. 15:58).

In the final analysis, resurrection faith is more than an attitude. It is a way of living made possible by radical trust in God. *Radical* is the needed word, for resurrection faith beckons our trust even and especially in those times and places where death's victory and sting seem indisputable. It is a way of living, for Paul indicates that resurrection faith excels in the "work" of God. Some traditions have posed false divisions between faith and work, as if one could be separated from the other. They cannot. Faith empowers the work. Work expresses the faith. That is not works righteousness. That is the message of Jesus, whose own incarnation of grace in ministry became the example for his commissioning us to "'let your light shine before others, so that they may see your good works and give glory to your Father in heaven'" (Matt. 5:16).

What is true of faith in general is especially true for resurrection faith. Clearly, God does not say we fashion our own resurrections. Even Jesus did not do that: God raised Jesus. Rather, the works of resurrection faith have to do with matching conduct and ethics with trust and hope. If we trust the power of life over death against all odds and appearances, we then find motivation to act undeterred by those odds and appearances. Deeds of justice and mercy become signs of the future in this present day. Lives of compassion and love assert the presence of God's realm in places where God seems anything but present. Resurrection faith commissions us to such labor, and the resurrected Christ is our assurance, our hope, our trust that we do not act in vain.

Do you believe that hope? And just as importantly, do you live that hope?

Resurrecting Life—and the Longing for Home

In considering the link between "resurrecting life" and hope as the "longing for home," the words of Augustine again come to mind: "You have made us for yourself, and our hearts are restless until they rest in you." If we consider that an accurate reflection of the core of spiritual life, then what we allude to in the language of resurrection is vital. Why? If God has made us for God's self, would God fashion something that is here one day and gone the next? To do so would make God's purposes in our creation fickle. We would be like the toy a child wishes for one day, only to grow bored with it the next so that it is no longer needed or wanted. God is not fickle. At least that is not the testimony of the biblical witness. In Old Testament terms, *hesed* is God's nature. Translated sometimes as "steadfast love," *hesed* also means a fierce loyalty that goes the extra mile to remain in relationship, to stay in covenant.

But how can relationship be maintained, how can God's *hesed* be exercised in covenant with us if death brings to an end all possibility of relationship? And if we speak of hope as longing for home and if by home we mean life lived in the presence and awareness of God, then death means ultimately the loss of all hope and with it home. Something has to give. Relationship with God has to cease at death, or death has to be breached to allow for relationship to continue in order that we might "rest in God." Which will it be?

"Thanks be to God, who gives us the victory through our Lord Jesus Christ." That is Paul's assessment of what yields: death is given its notice in the raising of Jesus. Our longing for home in God does not make us restless through these days on this side of the grave only to come to an abrupt and decisive end. Hope as our longing for home with God will be brought to fruition. We will rest in God. We begin to know and trust that now. We have experiences of such rest and home on this way we presently travel, though only in part.

What assures us of that hope and that home?
We have what the community of faith has always had:
An invitation to trust,
A message and a mystery to take to heart:
That Christ is risen—
Christ is risen indeed.
And death shall be no more.
So said Paul.
So said John Donne.
What say you?

Chapter 8

HOPE
CONFRONTING SEPARATION

Romans 8:31-39

Hope in God assumes that there is a Such,
and a participating One in this world:
this hope impels me forward in the time line of my life.

—Jan Seale

Childhood development specialists tell us that all children go through a phase of separation anxiety. A parent attempts to leave the room, whether to go to work or take a bathroom break, and the child cries and clings. After all, it is a scary thing for a toddler to imagine that the one who has been depended upon for nourishment, cleaning, and play will suddenly be gone. The anxiety gradually disappears over time as the child trusts the parent or caregiver to return. Older children who continue to struggle with this issue in severe ways suffer from separation anxiety disorder. For a few, the disorder persists or occurs in adulthood.

While separation anxiety disorder may affect a limited number of children and adults, the anxiety generated by separation is universal. We catch hints of it all through life. At school graduations we face the real possibility of no longer being in relationship with others who have formed our social group for years. We leave one job for another and feel a sadness for coworkers we will miss. Parents know the pangs of separation, from the first wave to a kindergartner off to school to living with an empty nest. Divorces may be uncontested, but they are never unaffecting.

And then there is death. It might seem odd that this book on hope did not end with the previous chapter on resurrection. After all, God has raised Jesus. "The strife is o'er, the battle done." Or is it?

Resurrection is not an end point in the life of faith. It is, if anything, a beginning point. Death may be behind Jesus, but it is still ahead of us. We face separation in its final form and in all manner of occurrences in between, not because we are sinful or lacking in faith but because we are human and created in God's image. We long for relationship with God and with one another. That is how God formed us; that is *why* God formed us. So if we are to live with faith and hope in this time, we need to confront the separations that come to us. We cannot deny them. In many ways we cannot escape them. But we can face them in the trust of One whose love promises both hope and home from which we cannot be separated.

If God Is for Us. . . .

Let's not rush to get past this word of Paul at the outset of the passage from Romans. "If God is for us . . ." is not a rhetorical question. And there is not just one reasonable answer.

"If God is for us." How might the folks trapped on the upper floors of the World Trade Center have answered in that terror of knowing there would be no way down or out alive? How might refugees in Darfur have answered as they tried in vain to hide from the militias who stalked and killed them? How might a parent answer whose child was the innocent victim of a drive-by shooter or a drunk driver or a sexual predator? "If God is for us" is not an easily made presumption in this world. It is, if anything, an act of extraordinary faith. So, is God for us?

During the time Paul wrote Romans, some gods in the Mediterranean area and Asia Minor went with the territory. Literally. That is, they were believed to be the god of this people or the god of that region, gods who basically sided with the hometown crowds. Such gods were for us as long as we belonged to the right group or offered the designated sacrifices to keep them happy. Such gods took our sides in wars and devastated our enemies. Such gods provided favorable economic status as long as our offerings were timely.

We might think we have advanced over these thousands of years beyond such primitive ideas of divine favor. History tells otherwise. "God for us" has been invoked in wars simultaneously on both sides of the battle lines without a tinge of conscience. The other day I watched a newscast as ministers prayed with fervor for God to lower the cost of gasoline in America. I am sure some pray-ers would argue that their concern was for the poor and the lopsided proportion the poor have to pay for fuel costs in relation to their total income. Still, is God's favor related to the price of crude on the futures market? Does the Holy One prefer the flag and ethnicity of one nation over against the value of their enemies' humanity? Is that the hope of God's favor that transforms the world?

Hardly. So then what does it mean to say that God is for us? Perhaps it will help if we keep those two terms clear: (1) God, (2) for us.

God. The God Paul affirms to be for us is not a tribal god. Good Jew that he is, Paul does not speak of God as the God of the Jews or the God of the Christians. Nor can we speak of God as the God of the West or the God of the church or the God of a particular affiliation. To speak of God is to speak of the One and only One who sets the tides in motion, who fashions genetic codes and black holes, who understands the language of a baby's coo as clearly as the expressions of our most gifted linguists and artists. God is the God of the universe, or God is not God—at least not the God of such hope as Paul seeks to affirm. Hope begins, in the thought of my friend Jan Seale in the opening quote, in the trust there is Such a One and that One not only participates in this world but does so in a way inclined to our good.

But Paul does not speak of God as a philosophical construct. The Holy One has revealed God's own self and love in the person of Jesus Christ. God has taken on the scandal of particularity, not because God is limited and limiting in grace and love. Rather, God has taken on the scandal of particularity in Jesus of Nazareth in order to make that grace and love not just a talking point but an incarnation. God has entered human life, so that we may trust and hope that the One who is "for us" knows us from the inside.

This God, this Incarnate One, Paul affirms to be "for us"—the whole of human creation. God "for us" means God is not manipulated into taking sides in the intramurals of human prejudice, whether we frame those prejudices with labels of religion or politics, country of origin or economic status, sexual orientation or hair color. God is for humanity. If God were not for us, there would have been no Incarnation. Why enter life as one you consider irredeemable? If God were not for us, the cross would be ludicrous. Why love the ultimately unloveable? If God were not for us, there would have been no creation of one drawn up from the dust (adamah), much less identification of that one with the very image of God.

We find it hard to wrap our minds, much less hearts, around the expansive view of the "us" God favors. Little wonder then that the Bible elsewhere employs the word mystery for an even broader understanding. Listen, for example, to this rendering of "mystery" in Ephesians.

> With all wisdom and insight [God] has made known to us the mystery of his will, according to his good pleasure that he set forth in Christ, as a plan for the fullness of time, to gather up all things in him, things in heaven and things on earth (Eph. 1:8-10).

Hope exceeds human destiny. Unless Ephesians is wrong, God's plan for humanity and all creation is for gathering, returning, homecoming.

Think about the hope we receive in Jesus Christ, a hope explored in the previous chapter on resurrection. Multiply that by all those whom God is for—and then for good measure toss in Ephesians' vision of all things gathered up in God. Can you imagine that? For in the imagining and the trusting comes the courage to live and act in hope of the Holy One, whom both cross and Easter declare is for us! Courage is the right word there, for courage is our true need in the midst of experiences and powers that inflict separation.

The Powers That Separate

Litanies, familiar parts of the church's liturgical tradition, often function as responsive readings or prayers. A common line may be repeated in response to words or prayers. Another meaning of litany has to do with listings. A "litany of complaints" might refer to a catalogue of grievances raised in public. In either case, litany usually does connote words spoken for all to hear. Litany is not private or exclusive knowledge. It is offered to the community and liturgically to God.

Twice in the Romans passage, Paul uses litanies. These are not litanies of praise or inventories of God's attributes. The first litany in verse 35 lists experiences that inflict separation. Some commentators noted that these experiences likely came out of Paul's own life (see also 2 Corinthians 11:24-27) as well as that of the early church. In other words, Paul does not base his case for hope on a situation of ease, nor does the community he addresses face an existence free of troubles. The gospel and our faith are neither our immunity to nor escape pod from life's hardships. In the case of Paul and the church, those hardships often arose as a direct result of the gospel and faith's expression. The second litany in verses 38-39 lists forces that may bring about experiences of separation. In these litanies, Paul names potential sources of separation as the first step in confronting them. In doing so, Paul invites us to do the same.

Naming such experiences and powers is not as simple as it sounds. Often the things that divide us and threaten to pull us apart are the very things we keep quiet about within the church. Consider the handling of clergy misconduct in congregations in the past: a quiet transfer of the offender, sometimes without censure. A shunning of the victim who takes the blame. Such silence only deepens the division and separation.

Naming such experiences and powers in the wider community can be no less risky and require no less courage. We shy away from discussing why individuals of color do not feel at home in the community. We do not want to come out and say that those evangelicals and fundamentalists would be better off in another church. In the wider political arena, those who would separate the world into "those who are not with us must be against us" are reluctant to hear that attitude named as anything but patriotism.

Naming the experiences and powers that threaten us with separation is only the first step. Confronting them with the gospel is the next. In my own understanding, that confrontation requires both a yes and a no. Paul does both in this passage.

The yes Paul offers comes in his affirmation of God's justification of us and Christ's intercession for us. Paul faces experiences and powers that threaten to separate us from hope with the positive affirmation that God has already spoken and acted to declare God's favor. And if that is so, who is to say otherwise? Paul does go on to identify those entities that say otherwise in his litanies. When we find ourselves in the midst of those experiences that cause us to question our standing, when we find ourselves faced with forces that seem to undo our standing before God, Paul declares we need to fall back on the fundamental assertion of this passage and the gospel itself. Who is qualified to bring charges against us if God is for us? Who is qualified to condemn us if Christ intercedes for us?

In addition to saying yes to the One who says yes to us, our confronting of that which would threaten us with separation also involves a negative. That is, we need to say no to some things. We need to say no to death's having the final word among us. We need to say no to every claim or threat whose appeal comes down to fear, for fear is little else than death in disguise. Paul argues that nothing can separate us from the love of God in Christ Jesus. We need to say no to anyone and anything that would tell us we are not valued children of God or that treats others as less than God's valued children. Such devaluation tries to separate human beings from that which is God-given. Only God can take away what God gives. As Paul has already reminded us, if God justifies—who is to condemn?

Hope's saying yes and saying no may occur in the political arena with stands taken for the sake of justice and compassion. When a loved one slips under the pall of Alzheimer's disease, we say yes to the hope that the individual remains a loved child of God; we say no to his or her state of being as the final state of existence. If nothing will separate us from the love of God, how can it otherwise be?

Paul reminds us that we do not need to give in to such powers and the separations they might otherwise threaten. We do not need to consider ourselves lost and adrift when we face situations that afflict us. In those situations, in the midst of those powers, we find our hope and life in Christ. And why is that a matter of hope and life? *"In all these things we are more than conquerors through him who loved us"* (emphasis added). When we live in Christ, the last word of our lives is not separation or even death: it is love.

The Last Word: Love

Judy and I recently bought two telescopes. I'm still trying to learn the difference between refracting and reflecting and when to use a Barlow and why you need an inverting lens. But on nights when marine air hasn't clouded over the sky by evening, we've gazed at the moon and stars and what we think have been planets. After we get experienced at using these new toys, we might figure out how to see what the ads on TV promise about being able to watch the moons of Jupiter or the rings of Saturn. Maybe. But no matter how many lenses we add or how skilled we get, I know already that neither we nor even the Hubble telescope will ever be able to see a place or an emptiness that lies outside the bounds or reach of God's love.

What goes for the universe stretching far around us holds true for the world around and within us. There is no place, no emptiness outside the reach of God's love: nowhere out there in the world, nowhere in here in the core of our individual existence. Now whether we hear that as bad news or good news depends on our image of God. If we view God as a vengeful deity whose only delight is to pounce on our mistakes and point out our errors and hold us accountable throughout eternity for any and every offense to holy being, then the God who is everywhere is a terrible burden and threat. During the Great Awakening in 1741, the Puritan preacher Jonathan Edwards preached of such a God in one of the most famous sermons in American history, "Sinners in the Hands of an Angry God."

> The God that holds you over the pit of hell, much as one holds a spider, or some loathsome insect over the fire, abhors you, and is dreadfully provoked: his wrath towards you burns like fire; he looks upon you as worthy of nothing else, but to be cast into the fire. . . . You have offended him infinitely more than ever a stubborn rebel did his prince; and yet it is nothing but his hand that holds you from falling into the fire every moment.[1]

If that reflects your view of God, then Psalm 139 would seem a nightmare:

> Where can I escape from your spirit?
>   Where flee from your presence?
> If I climb to heaven, you are there;
>   if I make my bed in Sheol, you are there. . . .
> Darkness is not too dark to you and night is as light as day.
> (vv. 7-9, 12; REB)

There is nowhere you can go where God is not. That is bad news for those whose knowledge of God is wrapped in fear. But that is good news for those whose knowledge of God is experienced in love—which is to say, experienced in Christ. In Jesus, God made love incarnate. John 3:16 does not begin "For God so *hated* the world"—no, the affirmation is "For God so *loved* the world." God's love defines what God seeks in and for this world. "There is nowhere you can go where God is not" means that there is nowhere you can go where you can be separated from God's love. And that is cause not for fear but for hope, a point made in the first epistle of John: "In love there is no room for fear; indeed love banishes fear" (4:18, REB). In Jesus Christ, we come face-to-face with the truth of God's ever-present love that refutes any and all attempts at separation or denial.

"I am convinced," Paul says, that nothing "will be able to separate us from the love of God in Christ Jesus our Lord." These words do not express softheaded romanticism or wishful thinking. They state how God has been revealed to us in the cross and raising of Jesus. In the Resurrection, God exposes death's fatal flaw: death relies on the power of fear. Fear relies on the threat of separation from loved ones, from the goodness of the created order in the experience of death from our very selves. Death claims it has the last word. God replies in the Resurrection that death's end has begun. Fear's reign has started to crack. Separation is not the final word. Life and love is the final word. Jesus knew the pain of separation on the cross—how else do we explain his cry, "My God, my God, why have you forsaken me?" From the perspective of the cross, from life lived on this side of the grave, that cry is understandable. It is ours as well. But it is a cry whose answer we find in God's raising of Jesus: nothing will finally separate us from my love. Nothing.

I too can at times be a literalist when it comes to the Bible. And I take Paul seriously when he says not "anything else in all creation will be able to separate us from the love of God in Christ Jesus our Lord." Not anything: no experience, no act of human will or rebellion that will prove an effective or absolute barrier to God's love. I am also a realist. Can we act in defiance or contradiction of God' love? Yes. God fashioned us with free wills, and freedom allows for the possibility of irresponsibility as well as responsibility. Can we deny or delay love by closing our lives to its possibilities and renewal? Absolutely. But in the end, when it comes down to a battle of wills between us and God or between the powers and principalities as Paul spoke of them and the power of God, guess who wins? *Nothing* can separate us from God's love. Not death, not Alzheimer's, not church conflicts, not terrorists or political demagogues who rely on climates of fear. Nothing.

God's love has the last word, and that word becomes our life and hope. It follows us to our journey's end, even as God's love promises to make of that end a new beginning for us and all creation. "I am convinced that neither death, nor life, nor angels, nor rulers, nor things present, nor things to come, nor powers, nor height, nor depth, nor anything else in all creation, will be able to separate us from the love of God in Christ Jesus our Lord."

Confronting Separation—and the Longing for Home

Perhaps no other part of this book relies so much on faith as this connection between hope as the longing for home and confronting the separations that come to us. Why? Those separations that come to us in life are real and powerful. The grief we suffer at the loss of a parent or spouse is no mere illusion. The loss of home or memory due to the ravages or war or illness are not inconsequential. To gloss over the power of such separations is to gloss over the meaning of Christ's incarnation. In entering this life, in knowing it as we know it, God in Christ has stamped what we experience now with value and purpose.

Our longing for home in God suffers pain in such separations, for in the gifts of this life—the gifts of human relationship and community—we catch glimpses of the home for which we were created and toward which we now move. So we grieve when any one of those gifts of human experience is lost to us and others.

But the separation is not final. The power of forces and authorities that would claim to control us because of their ability to inflict such separation is limited. That is faith's witness in this present age. It can be a defiant word when those separations are used to coerce us. It can be a word out of step with conventional wisdoms that intone the finality of such loss to us. It certainly is a word of faith, whose promise often seems at odds in a world where the reign of death seems so entrenched, so incontrovertible. Except—except for this.

God is for us and has revealed that favor in Jesus Christ.
God's favor in Christ invites us to live,
   not in denial of reality but in hope of transformation.
God's favor in Christ invites us to live *in Christ,*
   as those willing to trust love has the final word
   as those willing to trust grace has the final say
      in the home to which God will gather us and all.

Chapter 9

HOPE

LIVING GODWARD

Revelation 21:1-5

No more death, grief, crying, pain.
Everything will be transformed and made new.
How amazing is that?
—SHARON HARDING, *commenting on Revelation 21:1-5*

H*ow amazing is that?"* I recently read an article that urged the recovery of the original meaning of words like *awesome* and *amazing.* Today we use such expressions in the most routine of ways. We identify a piece of clothing as awesome. We term an experience that catches us only slightly off-guard as amazing. Such uses neglect the rather formidable beginnings of these words. *Awesome* related to standing in the presence of something Other than us that generated awe: a blend of fear, terror, and wonder. Often that something (or someone) allied with an experience of the holy. *Amazing,* as its spelling suggests, derives from *maze.* Unlike a labyrinth, whose intent is to lead you in and lead you out on a single trustworthy way, a maze intends to mislead you with dead ends and multiple choices of paths. To be a-mazed is to be in a situation where explanations run short, where one choice seems as good—or as bad—as another.

But there is another way of looking at *amazed,* one that may make my friend Sharon's comments about Revelation 21 even more telling. In English as in Greek, the opposite of a word may be created by adding an *a* for a prefix. For example, the opposite of a "theist" (one who believes in God) is an atheist. Apply that to the word *maze.* We might then understand the word *a-maze* as the feeling of astonishment that comes from *not* feeling caught up in a tangle of dead ends and false choices. Amazed could be the exhilaration generated by discovering our orientation.

That is exactly what makes Revelation 21:1-5 amazing. Mazes that have held us captive, experiences that have misled and tricked and created despair: all these things, in the language and hope of this text, will be "no more." This passage expresses extraordinary freedom and even more extraordinary trust. Its hope is that our longing for home will finally and ultimately have the way forward cleared of all obstacles. We do not live in its environs yet. But as we take this hope to heart and allow it to transform not only what we expect of the future but how (and why) we conduct ourselves as we do now, we are empowered to orient our lives Godward.

How amazing is that?

New

The promise of the new holds greatest appeal for those grown tired or weary of the old. I do not mean that in the sense in which we today sometimes buy into the marketing ploy of needing to have the latest and fastest and shiniest to replace what we have hardly used. I mean that in the sense of why a terminally ill patient may make the decision to unhook from all the appliances that artificially extend a life that has become mostly a fog of pain. I mean that in the sense of why folks may grasp for new ways of organizing community after being wearied by the ceaseless character assassination that passes for politics these days. I mean that in the sense of why a mother might take herself and her children out of an abusive relationship in the hope of finding something different, something humane, something new.

The promise of the new has greatest appeal to those grown tired or weary of the old in the sense that the author of Revelation first cast these words. Sometimes all we hear and see of the book of Revelation are the wildness of the visions. Or sometimes all we latch onto is its coded language so that we exhaust our time and energies identifying who the Antichrist is among us or how bar codes subtly fulfill the prophesied mark of the beast. And in the meantime we neglect to recognize or even acknowledge the original recipients to whom these words were addressed. They were a community suffering persecution, a community whose members transformed the meaning of the Greek word *martyr* from one who witnesses to faith to one who dies for faith. This community lived and suffered under the whims of an imperial political system that sought to enforce a rigid uniformity of allegiance under pain of death. In other words, they were a community grown understandably weary of the old world as it was, whose hope came in the promise of the "new."

The promise of the new, then and now, offers neither escape nor immunity from the old. Rather, it encourages faithful resistance to the old by declaring who holds the future. "Behold, I make all things new" (KJV) is how Revelation relays the word of hope from the One on the throne. Ironically, this promise of the new in Revelation is not at all new in the biblical witness. Time and again when God's people had fallen into hard places and the old oppressed with a rigor that threatened life and community, the word of the "new" consistently spoke hope. When a pharaoh arose over Egypt who did not know Joseph, God delivered the Israelites out of captivity and led them to a new land. When Israel languished in exile, the Isaiah tradition sounded hope by announcing God's invitational promise: "Do not remember the former things, or consider the things of old. I am about to do a new thing" (43:18-19). When the rebuilding of Jerusalem seemed long in coming, that same tradition offered words that may have been in the memory of Revelation 21's author: "I am about to create new heavens and a new earth" (65:17).

New heavens and new earth. Such is the promise of God to those who suffer old times and ways, who long for what is not yet—and in the eyes of some, for what can never be. One of the hard questions to face about such hope is this: what does the promise of the "new" mean for those of us grown quite comfortable and content with the old? What possible hope can the promise of the new bring to folks for whom this present age and its conditions are stacked in their (our) favor? After all, we might see how Revelation's promise of "all things new" would appeal to a refugee in a developing country or a homeless person in our midst or even the ones among us whose family or personal lives have been so wracked with tragedy or pain that anything new would be an improvement. But how does "all things new" appeal to those of us privileged with health and resources and stability of life? Would hope not be more of the same?

Here biblical hope surpasses mere optimism. Biblical hope recognizes and lives in the truth of that passage from Hebrews quoted in the prologue: "They confessed that they were strangers and foreigners on the earth, for people who speak in this way make it clear that they are seeking a homeland" (11:13-14). Biblical hope involves living as strangers and sojourners. A merely optimistic view of the future revolves around the baggage of what old stuff we get to carry from here. A hopeful view of the future centers on the promise of the new and the One who makes that possible. The story of the rich young ruler and Jesus illustrates the difference. Jesus invites this young man to set aside the accumulation of things for the sake of following. But for that individual the old gets in the way of the new. He at least has the integrity to recognize you can't have it both ways. To listen to some current purveyors of Christian hope marketed in "have it now" theologies of affluence and influence, where riches now preview riches later, you long for that young man's honesty. At least he leaves the gospel untouched rather than seeking to make it into his own image and favor.

The genuine hope to which God calls us is to the new. New heavens. New earth. All things new. Our home is not in the things we accumulate and surround ourselves with. We do not long in Christian hope for more of the same, only dished up eternally. Our longing is for the new. Our longing is for a home where we dwell fully in the renewing presence of God.

Tenting

In days when my back was more open to sleeping on the ground (or at least cushioned with an air mattress that, almost unfailingly, would deflate by morning), my wife, son, and I tent camped. It had the great advantage of portability. You didn't need paved roads and clearances required by motor homes or trailers. You didn't need large swaths of open ground to fit vehicles whose square footage exceeded our apartment at seminary. You just needed a tent and the willingness to live a day or two or more out there in the middle of it, whether "it" consisted of a forest or lakeside or desert setting. If they did nothing else, tents got you close and personal with the setting.

Portability. The sense of being right there in the middle of it. Tents provide that. Thanks to David, Solomon, and later Herod, we sometimes have forgotten that the Hebrew faith had its beginnings, not in rock-solid walls of temples but in tents whose sides were apt to flap about in the wind. And in Hebrew, wind and spirit are the same word.

Our origins are in "tented" faith, the ancient tradition of the God who chose to dwell among the people in tents. The older English word is *tabernacle*. Today we probably consider tabernacle as a synonym for a religious building. Certainly the Mormon Tabernacle (and its so-named and renowned choir) in Salt Lake City reinforces that popular understanding. But in its oldest meaning, tabernacle is simply a tent. The association of God and tabernacle came in the ark of the covenant's being housed in a tent. The ark represented God's presence, and so it brought a vivid image of God "living" in a tent. There is even the trace of a tradition in the Hebrew scriptures that suggests God's tabernacling was not because nobody had thought yet to build a temple. When David thinks God deserves better housing than that, God tells the prophet Nathan to set David straight:

> I have not lived in a house since the day I brought up the people of Israel from Egypt to this day, but I have been moving about in a tent and a tabernacle. Wherever I have moved about among all the people of Israel, did I ever speak a word with any of the tribal leaders of Israel,

whom I commanded to shepherd my people Israel, saying, "Why have you not built me a house of cedar?" (2 Sam. 7:6-7).

So what has all of this to do with hope and Revelation's promise of God's new and renewing presence in our midst? In Revelation 21:3, "home" and "dwell" translate the Greek word *skenoo* whose meaning as both a noun and verb is tabernacle or tent. "The home [tent] of God is among mortals. [God] will dwell [tent] with them" is a more literal translation of that verse. The God who had once been on the move with and right there in the midst of Israel's nomadic tents: that God will now pitch stakes and tabernacle among us again.

Put yourself in the situation of the original community addressed by Revelation. Given the suffering, the persecution, and the martyrdom we might justifiably wonder where God was in all of this. We might stand in fear of those impressive Roman temples and fortresses and consider how such power could be neutralized much less unseated. To this community Revelation speaks hope in the promise of God's choosing to tent with us. It is intriguing that the words chosen to express God's dwelling among us are not the "structure" words of dwelling available to the author in Greek. They are the "tent" words, the movement words. God's power is not in artificial edifices but in the ability to move freely in the making new of all things. Buildings are hard to move. They rarely budge. But the God who tabernacles is free to go wherever and to whomever the need may be.

Hope as symbolized in the new creation where God tents among us offers a tantalizing idea as well. If God tents among us, life lived in God's presence will not be immobile and staid. Home will be with One who continues to move unencumbered among us. God will resume a relationship with us in a more intimate way that, for the author of Revelation, hearkens back to earlier times and experiences of God that now go the heart—and hope—of this passage.

But how is God with us? In what actions does Revelation portray God's presence transforming us and all creation from the former things into the new things?

A clue to Revelation 21 and its vision of God's ultimate renewal comes in the opening chapter of John's Gospel: "The Word became flesh and lived among us" (v. 14). This verse affirms the significance of Jesus' life with us. It sets the stage for why the teachings and ministry of Jesus will be decisive for revealing the love of God and its invoking of our love for one another. But if we take a closer look at this verse, it asserts a powerful link with Revelation 21. The word translated "lived among" in John 1:14 is the same word in Revelation 21, verse 4: *skenoo*, "to tabernacle." The renewal of creation begins in the Word's "tenting" among us; that is, in the Word's joining us right here in the middle of life. God in Christ does not teach and save and renew from above or from afar. God in Christ tabernacles with us in the Word become flesh. And the good news begins.

Likewise, in the fulfillment of all things and the completion of the gospel's promise and hope, God tabernacles among us. For how or where else could God be near enough to wipe away tears? How or where else could God be close enough to ensure that mourning, crying, and pain will be no more? Not from some lofty and safe perch high above all the things that pain us, grieve us, and weigh us down. No, God comes; God tents among us in order to be in the intimacy of position and relationship to bring these promises to reality. Transformation and renewal do not come from without but from within. The future turns on where God will be found. And God will make home and set up camp among us.

Living Godward. . . and the Longing for Home

We have traveled long through these chapters to reach Revelation's vision of God's tabernacling among us. What have we encountered along this way?

- God's determination to covenant with all creation for the sake of life;

- the confession of wanderers who remind us where we have come from in order that we might know where and to whom we are heading;
- the Shepherd Psalm's assurance that we may trust God;
- the challenge of Isaiah's vision to see justice not only in the future's end but in the present's call;
- the surprise of the ones and the ways God blesses;
- the embrace and reconciliation of God's love;
- the raising of hope in the face of death through the resurrected Jesus;
- the summons to challenge powers that threaten separation with the word of God's undeniable favor;
- the vision of the end of all things that ushers in the beginning of all things through God's intimate presence among us.

We have been brought through these texts and stories to consider the ways and the One who comprise our home. Through them we have received the call to live Godward.

Living Godward implies a sense of direction—and it involves the recognition that the journey continues. These words and texts of hope are not meant to be beloved documents that lift our minds and spirits but leave our lives and actions untouched. Living Godward asserts the relationship of hope to discipleship. Hope is its motive, not its substitute. Like faith, hope without works is dead. Remember Roddy Hamilton's cautionary words at the beginning of this book about hope's being "wishy-washy?" Thinking Godward without living Godward is just that.

But hope is also not limited to a by-product of human endeavor. At its foundation is the gracious love and sovereign power of God. Even when we or others fail or fall short of our calling to embody the works of God, hope does not fail. God does not fail. God's purposes for us and for creation will come to pass. Consider again this chapter's text, and the community it originally addressed. The empire's perse-

cution of the church, deadly as it was, ultimately failed. The enemies
of justice and compassion in this world, past and present and future,
will ultimately fail. We cannot prove that in the midst of such experiences; we can only witness to the hope we have been given in God.
God's sovereign realm will not be turned aside. God's grace and God's
love will have the final say. Our home as gift and promise is secure.
So now it remains for us to live Godward in the midst, not the denial,
of these days. We are to live in such a way that our lives become the
signs and sources of what has been promised and of the character of
the God who has promised them.

Someday we will dwell in that home. Someday the words Robert
Louis Stevenson chose as the epitaph for his grave will be ours:

> Here he lies, where he longed to be;
> Home is the sailor, home from the sea,
> And the hunter home from the hill.

But for us the first line will be this: here we live where we longed
to be. In the presence of God we will finally and fully live in that
home for which faith longs.

Until then we live Godward in the hope we are given, in the discipleship to which we are called, in the community into which we are
gathered, in the Spirit's gift with which we are empowered. It seems
fitting to end this book with an affirmation, a liturgy, of hope. Offer
it to declare your trust. Offer it to encourage your service. Offer it to
praise the One who is our home.

> Hope grounds us in a covenant struck by God's grace,
> and we live Godward in our covenant relationships now.

> Hope confesses God's story to be the saving part of our story,
> and we live Godward as we remember whose we are.

> Hope trusts in God's leading upon all the paths we travel,
> and we live Godward by renouncing fear and trusting God.

> Hope anticipates God's restoring of justice in all creation,
> and we live Godward as we seek God's justice in our time.

Hope orients us by the ones and ways God blesses,
and we live Godward by heeding the bearings of God's blessing.

Hope finds all loved by a God prodigal in grace,
and we live Godward by receiving and offering others that grace.

Hope resurrects life in light of God's raising of Jesus,
and we live Godward as those who no longer fear death nor life.

Hope confronts separation with the word of God's favor and love,
and we live Godward by entrusting ourselves to the power of grace.

Hope promises God's dwelling with us,
and we live Godward by trusting holy presence
    in this time and for all time.

Appendix 1: Spiritual Exercises

This section provides five daily exercises for each chapter of this book. The exercises follow an ancient practice for engaging scripture known as *lectio divina* ("holy reading"). It is important to practice this discipline in a time and place that is conducive to reflection and prayer. The suggested time for each of these exercises is ten to fifteen minutes. As you become used to the process, you may find yourself wanting to spend more time doing so. The practice of *lectio divina* used here will involve five elements (one per exercise each week):

Reading. This is not a speed read through the scripture but an unhurried engagement with its words and images, opening to the movement of God's Spirit through it.

Meditation. Specific words, images, and ideas will be highlighted for deeper immersion in the passage.

Prayer. Out of encounter with the scripture and its revealings of God (and ourselves) comes our response in prayer as "heartfelt conversation with God."

Action. This segment encourages us to move out into service and discipleship, grounded in the word engaged and the God encountered.

Contemplation. The sabbath element of *lectio divina*, we rest in the presence of God, opening ourselves to God's peace and renewal.

Traditionally *lectio divina* focuses on scripture. While these exercises are grounded in the scripture highlighted for specific chapters, they will regularly bring in parts of the chapters' readings or themes. In doing so these practices hope to weave the texts and the chapters' reflections on them more closely with your own experiences and your own call to live with hope.

1 Hope: Grounding in Grace

Day One—Reading

- Read Genesis 9:8-17 slowly and *silently* one time through.

- Ask yourself: What may God be seeking to reveal to me through this passage?

- Read Genesis 9:8-17 slowly and *aloud* one time through.

- Ask yourself: What do I experience of hope and grace in these words?

- Consider the day ahead (or behind, depending on when you do this reading). Read the passage a third time, keeping in mind those experiences and anticipations.

- Offer a brief prayer of thanks for this word, for this day, and for God's grace in both.

Day Two—Meditation

- Read Genesis 9:8-17. Identify words and phrases that seem especially critical to you or ones that raise questions (list them on a separate sheet of paper or in your journal). Consider why those words and phrases caught your attention. Make notes for later reference.

- With those words and phrases in mind, glance through chapter 1 and find where they are mentioned. How do the reflections about them in the chapter relate to what caught your eye in the reading of the scripture? Add those thoughts to ones noted before.

- Seek the Spirit's guidance in integrating these thoughts with this day's experiences.

Day Three—Prayer

- Glance over Genesis 9:8-17. Recall your thoughts, and read over the notes made in the previous two exercises. Then be in a spirit and attitude of prayer.

- Bring to this time those remembrances and associations from the scripture and the chapter. Offer the thoughts and questions to God.
- Bring to this time a willingness to listen. Find yourself comfortable with silence.
- Move between prayers generated by these readings with prayers that grow out of this day. Listen to connections between them as you may be led.

Day Four—Action

- Glance over Genesis 9:8-17 and chapter 1 of the book.
- Recall the question asked in the first exercise: What may God be seeking to reveal to me through this passage? Take that question a step farther: What may God be seeking you to do as a result of this passage or its accompanying chapter?
- Choose one action. One example could be (but not limited to) some action related to greater care and more responsible stewardship of the environment. Do not limit yourself to something that can only be done in one day or only by you. Choose something that you at least *begin* today.
- Seek God's leading and presence in this action you will take.

Day Five—Contemplation

- Reflect briefly on the previous four exercises and your actions in response.
- Offer a prayer of thanks for opportunities to read and respond and for where God has led you this week through those reflections and activities.
- Rest for a while in a spirit of gratitude and expectancy in God's presence. Be at ease. Enjoy the gift of being held in an environment of grace. When you are ready, leave this "sanctuary" trusting your life to be grounded in God's grace.

2   Hope: Confessing Our Story

Day One—Reading

- Read Deuteronomy 26:1-12 slowly and silently, one time through.

- Ask yourself: What may God be seeking to reveal to me through this passage?

- Read Deuteronomy 26:1-12 slowly but aloud one time through.

- Ask yourself: How does this passage tell my story? When has God heard and seen me?

- Consider the day ahead (or behind, depending on when you do this reading). Read the passage a third time, keeping in mind those experiences and anticipations.

- Offer a brief prayer of thanks for this word, for this day, and for God's presence with you.

Day Two—Meditation

- Read Deuteronomy 26:1-12. Identify words and phrases that stand out (list them on a separate sheet of paper or in your journal).

- Glance through chapter 2 and find where those words or themes appear. How does the chapter's reflections about them relate to their use in the scripture and to hope?

- Imagine you had to paraphrase the confession ("A wandering Aramean. . . milk and honey") from your own experiences. What would you write as your story? Write it.

- Seek the Spirit's guidance as you anticipate this day in light of your story and this story.

Day Three—Prayer

- Skim Deuteronomy 26:1-12 and chapter 2. Recall your thoughts, and read over the notes made in the previous two exercises. Be in a spirit and attitude of prayer.

- Bring to this time those associations from the scripture and the chapter. Pray for where you are on life's journey. Pray for individuals and groups in vulnerable situations and for openness to God's working through you on their behalf.

- Come with a willingness to listen. Find yourself comfortable with silence.

- Offer gratitude for the good God brings to you and the good you may bring to others.

Day Four—Action

- Focus on Deuteronomy 26:11-12 and "Confession Enacted: Hospitality and Justice" (pages 34–37).

- Listen to these words and remember the vulnerable ones prayed for in the previous exercise. What may God be seeking you to do on their behalf?

- Choose one specific action. If possible, ensure that it involves you not simply in action taken for someone or a group but action that brings you into community with them . . . and/or opens your community to them. Do not limit yourself to something that can only be done in one day or only by you. Choose something that you at least *begin* today. Enter this action with hope.

- Seek God's leading and presence in the action you will take.

Day Five—Contemplation

- Reflect briefly on the previous four exercises and your action(s) in response.

- Offer a prayer of thanks for God's inclusion of you and others in this story of grace enacted, community created, and mission imparted.

- Rest for a while in a spirit of gratitude and expectancy in God's presence. Be at ease. Enjoy the gift of being part of the community God calls to life and partners with in service. When you are ready, leave this "sanctuary" in hope.

3   Hope: Trusting God's Leading

Day One—Reading

- Read Psalm 23 slowly and silently one time through.

- Ask yourself: What may God be seeking to reveal to me through this passage?

- Read Psalm 23 slowly but aloud one time through.

- Ask yourself: When and how have I experienced God's leading in my life? What has made it easy or difficult to trust that leading?

- Consider the day ahead (or behind, depending on when you do this reading). Read the passage a third time, keeping in mind those experiences and anticipations.

- Offer a brief prayer of thanks: for this word, for this day, for trust in God's leading.

Day Two—Meditation

- Read Psalm 23. Identify words and phrases that strike you in some special way. Make note of them and something as to why they attract your attention.

- Glance through chapter 3 and find where those words or their themes appear. How does the chapter reflect on their use in the scripture and/or their relationship to hope?

- The psalm uses a vocation contemporary to that day (shepherd) to serve as a metaphor for God's leading. Choose an image from your life or modern experience that conveys something of God's leading. Describe in words or art the connection between that image and God's leading . . . and your trust of God.

- Be open to the Spirit's guidance as you seek such leading and offer such trust in this day.

Day Three—Prayer

- Glance through Psalm 23 and chapter 3. Recall your thoughts, and read over the notes made in the previous two exercises. Be in a spirit and attitude of prayer.

- Bring to prayer a willingness to listen. Find yourself comfortable with silence.

- Bring to prayer what these readings have stirred in you. Pray for specific needs of God's leading and the ability to trust God.

- Entrust any fear you have this day to the care of God.

Day Four—Action

- Skim through Psalm 23 and chapter 3, especially the section "Even Though . . ." (pages 45–48).

- What action might you take that evidences both your trust of God's leading and your denying fear its power over your life?

- Choose one specific action. It could be a no to some fear or a yes to an action related to faith you have contemplated but never taken. Do not limit yourself to something that can be done in one day or only by you. Choose something that you can *begin* today.

- Seek God's leading and presence in this action you will take.

Day Five—Contemplation

- Reflect briefly on the previous four exercises and your action(s) taken in response.

- Offer a prayer of thanks for God's shepherding care. Reflect on the gift to be able to trust that leading and to know God's presence as dependable even in the face of fear.

- Rest for a while in a spirit of gratitude and expectancy in God's presence. Be at ease. Enjoy the gift of knowing God's presence around you and ahead of you. When you are ready, leave this time by trusting yourself to God's leading in this day.

4   Hope: Restoring Justice

Day One—Reading

- Read Isaiah 65:17-25 slowly and silently one time through.

- Ask yourself: What may God be seeking to reveal to you through this passage?

- Read Isaiah 65:17-25 slowly but aloud one time through.

- Ask yourself: What do I hear this text affirming about justice; about hope?

- Consider the day ahead (or behind, depending on when you do this reading). Read the passage a third time, keeping in mind those experiences and anticipations.

- Offer a prayer of thanks for this word, for this day, for the hope of God's justice.

Day Two—Meditation

- Read Isaiah 65:17-25. Identify words and phrases that stand out (list them on a separate sheet of paper or in your journal).

- Glance through chapter 4 and find where those words or themes appear. How does the chapter's reflections about them relate to their use in the scripture and to hope?

- Write your own anticipation of how God's "new heavens and new earth" will restore justice. Be specific. Reflect on the hopes you have identified.

- Seek the Spirit's guidance as you enter this day's experiences with an eye open to places and persons in need of such justice restored.

Day Three—Prayer

- Glance through Isaiah 65:17-25 and chapter 4. Be in a spirit and attitude of prayer.

- Bring to prayer a willingness to listen. Find yourself comfortable with silence.

- Bring to prayer what these readings have stirred in you. Pray for specific needs of God's justice in your community and in the world at large. Invite the Spirit's guidance of you and your faith community to be witnesses to and instruments of such justice.

Day Four—Action

- Focus on Isaiah 65:17-25 and "No More" (pages 55–57).
- Ask yourself: What is within my God-given power to do now for the sake of justice?
- Choose one specific action. It could enact a yes to some positive aspect of justice. It could also be an act of defiant "no more" to some present injustice. But choose something that you at least *begin* today. Act with hope in God's justice.
- Seek God's leading and presence in this action you will take.

Day Five—Contemplation

- Reflect briefly on the previous four exercises and your action(s) in response.
- Offer a prayer of thanks for the hope and promise of new heavens and new earth where justice is fully restored. Reflect on the empowering possibilities of that vision.
- Rest for a while in a spirit of gratitude and expectancy in God's presence. Be at ease. Enjoy the gift of being part of the movement toward wholeness and peace for all of creation in Christ. When you are ready, leave this "sanctuary" in hope, energized by the promise of justice restored to be a living sign of that restoration.

5 Hope: Orienting to God's Blessing

Day One—Reading

- Read Matthew 5:3-12 and Luke 6:20-21, 24-26 silently and slowly one time through.

- Ask yourself: What may God be seeking to reveal to me through this passage?

- Read Matthew 5:3-12 and Luke 6:20-21, 24-26 slowly but aloud one time through.

- Ask yourself: What do I hear of the ways and the ones blessed of God?

- Consider the day ahead (or behind, depending on when you do this reading). Read the passage a third time, keeping in mind those experiences and anticipations.

- Offer a brief prayer of thanks for this word, for this day, and for God's blessing.

Day Two—Meditation

- Read Matthew 5:3-12 and Luke 6:20-21, 24-26. Identify words and phrases that seem especially critical to you or ones that raise questions (list them on a separate sheet of paper or in your journal). Reflect on why those words and phrases caught your attention. Make notes for later reference.

- Glance through chapter 5 with those words and phrases in mind, and find where they may be used. In the chapter, how do the reflections about them or the themes they suggest relate to what caught your eye in the reading of the scripture? Add those thoughts to those noted before.

- Seek the Spirit's guidance in being attentive to these ideas within this day's experiences.

Day Three—Prayer

- Glance over Matthew 5:3-12 and Luke 6:20-21, 24-26 and chapter 5. Recall your thoughts, and read over your notes from the previous two exercises. Then be in a spirit and attitude of prayer.

- Bring to this time those remembrances and associations from the scripture and the chapter. Offer your thoughts and questions to God.

- Bring to this time a willingness to listen. Find yourself comfortable with silence.

- Move between prayers generated by these readings with prayers that grow out of this day. Listen and seek the Spirit's leading.

Day Four—Action

- Review briefly Matthew 5:3-12 and Luke 6:20-21, 24-26 and the final two paragraphs in "Blessed or Happy" (pages 65–66).

- Ask yourself: What may God be seeking to reveal to me through this passage? Then go a step farther: What may God be seeking me to do in response to the blessings and the blessed of God?

- Choose one action to live out one of these Beatitudes for the sake of someone who needs to know he or she is blessed of God. You need not limit yourself to something that can only be done in one day or only by you. Choose something that you *begin* today.

- Seek God's leading and presence in this action of bringing God's blessing to another.

Day Five—Contemplation

- Reflect on the previous four exercises and your action(s) in response.

- Offer a prayer of thanks for the blessings of God for creation. Bring to awareness the ways in which God has blessed your life through God's Spirit and others.

- Rest for a while in a spirit of gratitude and expectancy in God's presence. Be at ease. Enjoy the grace of knowing that God seeks blessing for you and through you. When you are ready, leave this "sanctuary" in the joy of God's blessings.

6   Hope: Finding Ourselves Loved

Day One—Reading

- Read Luke 15:1-3, 11-32 slowly and silently one time through. Ask yourself: What may God be seeking to reveal to me through this passage?

- Read Luke 15:1-3, 11-32 slowly but aloud one time through.

- Ask yourself: What does this text affirm about my own experiences of and longings for love?

- Consider the day ahead (or behind, depending on when you do this reading). Read the passage a third time, keeping in mind those experiences and anticipations.

- Offer a prayer of thanks for this word, for this day, for God's holding you in love.

Day Two—Meditation

- Read Luke 15:1-3, 11-32. Identify words and phrases that stand out (list them on a separate sheet of paper or in your journal).

- Glance through chapter 6 and find where those words or themes appear. How does the chapter's reflections about them relate to their use in the scripture and to hope?

- Recall an experience when you were a returning prodigal. Now consider an experience when you were a resentful elder . . . a welcoming parent. Choose one role, and journal your thoughts about that experience. Reflect on how that experience shaped your life and faith and affected your awareness of being loved.

- Seek the Spirit's guidance as you enter this day; keep an eye open to places and persons in need of finding themselves loved.

Day Three—Prayer

- Skim Luke 15:1-3, 11-32 and chapter 6. Be in a spirit of prayer.

- Bring to prayer a willingness to listen. Find yourself comfortable with silence.

- Bring to prayer what these readings and exercises have stirred in you this week. Pray for those in your circle of friends, family, and church who long for the assurance of being loved—including yourself. Invite the Spirit's guidance of you and your faith community to be instruments through whom God's love might flow.

Day Four—Action

- Review Luke 15:1-3, 11-32 and "A House Divided . . . and Divided . . . and Divided" (pages 76–78).

- Reflect on divisions—in your community, church, or family— that stand in the way of the exercise of love. Ask yourself: What might I be able to do in order to bear witness to love in the face of that division?

- Choose one action. Do not assume it will mend all wounds and heal all separations. But let it clearly express or embody love that defies the breaches in relationship and says that love offers the possibility of reconciliation. Choose something that you *begin* today. Act with hope, act with love.

- Seek God's leading and presence in the action you will take.

Day Five—Contemplation

- Reflect briefly on the previous four exercises and your action(s) in response.

- Offer a prayer of thanks for the love with which God holds you and all creation.

- Rest for a while in a spirit of gratitude and expectancy in God's presence. Be at peace. Enjoy the gift of knowing love is at the core of life, and God's gracious welcome is the destination and hope of creation and reconciliation. When you are ready, leave this "sanctuary" in hope, knowing God seeks us with arms wide open in loving welcome.

7 Hope: Resurrecting Life

Day One—Reading

- Read 1 Corinthians 15:12-26, 55-58 slowly and silently one time through.

- Ask yourself: What may God be seeking to reveal to me through this passage?

- Read 1 Corinthians 15:12-26, 55-58 slowly but aloud one time through.

- Ask yourself: What does resurrection hope mean in my life?

- Consider the day ahead (or behind, depending on when you do this reading). Read the passage a third time, keeping in mind those experiences and anticipations.

- Offer a prayer of thanks for this word and this day in the light of resurrection hope.

Day Two—Meditation

- Read 1 Corinthians 15:12-26, 55-58. Identify words and phrases that seem especially critical to you or that raise questions (list them on a separate sheet of paper or in your journal). Reflect on why those words and phrases caught your attention. Make notes for later reference.

- Glance through chapter 7 with those words and phrases in mind, and find where they may be used. In the chapter, how do the reflections about them or the themes they suggest relate to what caught your eye in the reading of the scripture? Add those thoughts to those noted before.

- Seek the Spirit's guidance in being attentive to these ideas in this day's experiences.

Day Three—Prayer

- Glance over 1 Corinthians 15:12-26, 55-58 and chapter 7. Read over the notes made in the earlier exercises. Enter into prayer.

- Bring to this time those remembrances and associations from the text and the chapter. Offer your thoughts and questions to God.
- Bring to this time a willingness to listen and be in silence.

Day Four—Action

- Review briefly 1 Corinthians 15:12-26, 55-58 and the final three paragraphs in "Taunts and Commissions" (pages 95–96).
- Recall the question asked in the first exercise: What may God be seeking to reveal to me through this passage? Take that question a step farther: What may God be seeking me to do in response to the hope and commission we are given in resurrection faith?
- Consider one action by which you can live out resurrection's promise that your labor will not be in vain. You need not limit yourself to something that can be done in one day or only by you. Choose something that you *begin* today.
- Seek God's leading and presence in this work spurred by resurrection hope.

Day Five—Contemplation

- Reflect on the previous exercises and your action(s) in response.
- Offer a prayer of thanks for God's raising of Jesus and the hope that act brought to you and to all. Be mindful of how that changes life in the face of death and fear.
- Rest for a while in a spirit of gratitude and expectancy in God's presence. Be at ease. Enjoy the grace of knowing that God seeks blessing for you and through you. When you are ready, leave this "sanctuary" in the hope of resurrection faith.

8   Hope: Confronting Separation

Day One—Reading

- Read Romans 8:31-39 slowly and silently one time through.

- Ask yourself: What may God be seeking to reveal to me through this passage?

- Read Romans 8:31-39 slowly but aloud one time through.

- Ask yourself: How does this text confront fears generated by separation with the word of God's favor and love?

- Consider the day ahead (or behind, depending on when you do this reading). Read the passage a third time, keeping in mind those experiences and anticipations.

- Offer a prayer of thanks for this word, for this day, for the God who is for you.

Day Two—Meditation

- Read Romans 8:31-39. Identify words and phrases that stand out (list them on a separate sheet of paper or in your journal).

- Glance through chapter 8 and find where those words or themes appear. How does the chapter's reflections about them relate to their use in the scripture and to hope?

- Divide a sheet of paper in half. On one side, write down your fears (and experiences) of separation. On the other side, note how the word of God's favor and love might speak to each of those in a way that brings you hope.

- Seek the Spirit's guidance to live with courage and hope in the face of separations.

Day Three—Prayer

- Skim Romans 8:31-39 and chapter 8. Be in a spirit and attitude of prayer.

- Bring to prayer a willingness to listen. Find yourself comfortable with silence.

- Pray for those in your circle of friends, family, and church who face difficult experiences of separation or who may wonder whether God truly is for them. Pray for comfort, guidance, and strength when those experiences and/or wonderings are your own. Be open to the way the Spirit might use you to affirm God's favor for another.

Day Four—Action

- Focus on Romans 8:31-39 and the final two paragraphs under "The Powers That Separate" (pages 104–105).
- Ask yourself: What fears or powers do I need to say no to, and what hope and expression of love do I need to say yes to in my life?
- Choose one action. It could enact a no to some threat based on separation. It could demonstrate a yes to a concrete expression of God's favor for another individual or group. It could accomplish something of both.
- Seek God's leading and presence in the action you will take.

Day Five—Contemplation

- Reflect briefly on the previous four exercises and your action(s) in response.
- Offer a prayer of thanks for the God who is for you and from whose love nothing can separate you.
- Rest for a while in a spirit of gratitude and expectancy in God's presence. Be at peace. Know that no experience of separation has within itself the power to sever you from God's love and favor. Draw strength and fresh courage from that hope. When you are ready, leave this "sanctuary" in hope, knowing God in Christ has made clear that grace will not be denied.

9 Hope: Living Godward

Day One—Reading

- Read Revelation 21:1-5 slowly and silently one time through.

- Ask yourself: What may God be seeking to reveal to me through this passage?

- Read Revelation 21:1-5 slowly but aloud one time through.

- Ask yourself: What hope do these words call me to trust and live out in my life?

- Consider the day ahead (or behind, depending on when you do this reading). Read the passage a third time, keeping in mind those experiences and anticipations.

- Offer a prayer of thanks for this word, for this day, and for God's presence in both.

Day Two—Meditation

- Read Revelation 21:1-5. Identify words and phrases that seem especially critical to you or ones that raise questions (list them on a separate sheet of paper or journal). Reflect on why those words and phrases caught your attention. Make notes for later reference.

- Glance through chapter 9 with those words and phrases in mind and find where they may be used. How do the reflections about them in the chapter relate to what caught your eye in the reading of the scripture? Add those thoughts to those noted before.

- Seek the Spirit's guidance in integrating these thoughts within your conduct.

Day Three—Prayer

- Glance through Revelation 21:1-5. Recall your thoughts, and read over the notes made in the previous two exercises. Then be in a spirit and attitude of prayer.

- Bring to this time remembrances and associations from the scripture and the chapter. Offer your thoughts and questions to God.

- Come with a willingness to listen. Find yourself comfortable with silence.
- Move between prayers generated by these readings with prayers that grow out of this day; listen to connections between them as you may be led.

Day Four—Action

- Reflect on Revelation 21:1-5 and chapter 9 of this book.
- Recall the question asked in the first exercise: What may God be seeking to reveal to me through this passage? Take that question a step farther: What may God be seeking me to do as a result of this passage or its accompanying chapter?
- Choose an action. One example could be (but not limited to) an action related to offering your presence, support, and advocacy to those who face pain and grief or who even may suffer for their faith or values. Do not limit yourself to something that can only be done in one day or only by you. Choose something that you *begin* today.
- Seek God's leading and presence in the action you will take.

Day Five—Contemplation

- Reflect briefly on the previous four exercises and your actions in response.
- Offer a prayer of thanks for opportunities to read and respond and for where God has led you this week through those reflections and activities.
- Rest for a while in a spirit of gratitude and expectancy in God's presence. Be at ease. Enjoy the gift of knowing the promise and current experience of God's transforming presence in your life and in all creation. When you are ready, leave this "sanctuary" in a spirit of commitment to live Godward through hope that takes shape in your life's conduct.

Appendix 2: Leader's Guide

Introduction

These suggested session outlines have been developed to aid groups who use *Hope: Our Longing for Home*. The study would consist of nine sessions, one per chapter. The process relies upon participants' reading the chapter to be covered and doing its spiritual exercises in the week *prior* to your gatherings. Make sure participants have the books at least one week before the first session, with instructions to read the prologue and chapter 1 and to do the spiritual exercises for chapter 1 in the back of the book. Consider adding a tenth session at the beginning of the study as an introduction. The introductory session can provide an opportunity for initial community building, general conversation about hope, distribution of materials, a walk-through of the book's structure, and instructions about the weekly readings and exercises. Reading and discussing each section of the prologue would outline a format for accomplishing the above.

The core of this group study will be based on the participants' work on these exercises that reflect on and invite action based on the week's scripture and reading. Whether you have an introductory session or not, be sure to convey the importance of doing the spiritual exercises. *Also* include the spiritual exercises for each chapter as part of your preparation to lead as well as your own participation in reflecting on these chapters and their scripture texts.

Each session will consist of suggestions for PREPARING, GATHERING, ENCOUNTERING, REFLECTING, SUPPORTING, and CLOSING.

PREPARING outlines ideas for readying the meeting space, gathering needed materials, and your own personal preparation to be done before the session.

GATHERING will offer ideas for worship and an activity that will introduce the theme.

ENCOUNTERING will engage the scripture text for the week.

REFLECTING considers the chapter and issues or questions arising out of the spiritual exercises of the past week. Do not gloss over or rush through this time. It may well present unexpected perspectives or thought-provoking considerations not anticipated in the session guide.

SUPPORTING will review the actions of hope elicited by the Day Four spiritual exercises and consider how those individual actions might be supported or joined by others.

CLOSING summarizes and reflects on the group experience, makes any assignments, and closes with a form of prayer and/or commissioning.

These session outlines are not word-for-word instructions that cannot be veered from. Feel free to adapt, adjust, and/or add to the suggestions based on the needs and experiences of your group. The suggested session length is 45 minutes. As a rule of thumb, consider the following times for each element of the session:

GATHERING	5 minutes
ENCOUNTERING	10–15 minutes
REFLECTING	10–15 minutes
SUPPORTING	10 minutes
CLOSING	5 minutes

Consider using any extra time in the areas of ENCOUNTERING, REFLECTING, and/or SUPPORTING.

For Every Session

MEETING SPACE

If possible, arrange participants' chairs in a circle around the worship center. Or, place the worship center at the open end of chairs set in the form of a horseshoe. In the CLOSING activities, instructions to "gather" around the worship center will have participants standing (as they are able).

PREPARATION

While you may not use all of these materials in every session, you will want to have them on hand for general use: newsprint and markers, blank paper and pens or pencils, sticky notes, Bibles (different translations would be helpful).

GATHERING

Bench or table with candle for use as a worship center. Suggestions for items to be placed on it will be made for each session.

ENCOUNTERING

You will *always* read the scripture for the week. A suggested method will be made each session.

REFLECTING

A repeated process for reviewing the chapter and spiritual exercise work will be used each week with little modification in this guide. It will be important to listen to the flow of conversation within this process to determine your group's points of emphasis.

SUPPORTING

Participants identify the action(s) generated by the Day Four spiritual exercise. Discuss how and where folks might work as a whole or in small groups to support one another and perhaps work together.

CLOSING

Summary and comments on session followed by an act of worship

1   Hope: Grounding in Grace

PREPARING

Materials: Pictures of people (variety of ages, ethnicities, settings) and animals, a globe or a photo of Earth taken from space; place on or around the worship center. Name tags (*not* the adhesive ones) for use throughout study.

Personal: This session affirms hope's grounding in the grace of God as revealed in the covenant God enters with all creation in Genesis 9. Where have you experienced or struggled with God's grace for you and/or for creation? What understandings of grace and hope do you find affirmed or challenged in this week's scripture and chapter?

GATHERING

Welcome participants and give them name tags to fill out and wear. The use of name tags will be important if this group has not met together on a regular basis before.

Light the candle on the worship center, and invite participants to look over the items on display on or around the worship center. Suggest that they identify silently the one that most draws their attention. Ask: **What might that picture or symbol suggest about hope or grace?** As they feel led, have participants offer a single sentence that identifies the item and makes connection to hope and/or grace. Invite participants to suggest what all of these items have in common.

Offer these or similar words in prayer:

> **God of all creation, all things draw life from you; all hope comes from you. Remind us of and renew us in the breadth of your grace. Amen.**

ENCOUNTERING

Form three groups to represent (1) Noah and his family, (2) all other living things, and (3) the earth. Have the groups stand apart in three corners of the room. Indicate that you will read the Genesis passage aloud. Tell the groups that when they hear the one(s) they represent named as part of God's covenant, the group is to come and stand by the worship center. Read aloud so all can hear Genesis 8:21-22; 9:8-17. Pause to allow groups to come to the worship center as they hear themselves included in God's covenant.

Afterward, discuss:

- How did you feel as you waited to hear your group included?
- Had your group not been included, what would that have meant in terms of hope?
- What does this passage reveal about hope, grace, and those named as recipients?

REFLECTING

Ask participants to reflect on chapter 1 and the spiritual exercises (holding off, at this point, on the Day Four choices of action). Do so by asking them to share with the group what spoke most deeply to them regarding affirmations, questions, disagreements, or new insights.

If you have as many as twelve persons, form small groups to allow individuals more time to speak.

Discuss ways in which these readings and exercises addressed participants' own understanding and experience of being grounded in grace. Ask: **In what ways does (or might) this congregation ground persons in grace?**

SUPPORTING

Ask participants to identify their chosen actions in response to the Day Four spiritual exercise. Do this by inviting individuals to write those choices on newsprint or, with a smaller group, going around the circle and doing so. Discuss how and where folks might combine efforts, either as the whole group or in small groups, to support one another and perhaps work together on one or more of the actions identified. If possible, use part of this time to plan or even do some of this common work.

CLOSING

Gather the group at the worship center. Remember the experience of listening to the Genesis story and being named and gathered as part of God's covenant. Look once again at the photos and symbols on the worship center. Say: **Everything there, everyone in this room, has been named by God as a covenant partner. All are grounded in grace. That is our hope, for that is God's gift.**

Close by offering the final lines of chapter 1 (page 26) as a responsive commissioning. You begin with the first line ("God's covenant is with you. . .") The group responds with the second line ("God's covenant is with every living creature. . .") and continues to read responsively the remaining lines.

2   Hope: Confessing Our Story

PREPARING

Materials: Family or church photo albums, a history of your church (if available), storybooks; place all of these on or around the worship center. Name tags.

Personal: This session explores how our stories of faith and community remind us not only of our past but the basis and character of our hope. Recall a story told about your parents or grandparents (or earlier) that has shaped your self-understanding. What enables that story to do so? Where do you see the connections between the stories of faith, biblical and congregational and personal, and Christian hope?

GATHERING

Welcome participants and hand out the name tags made last week. Introduce any visitors or newcomers, and ask them to make and wear a name tag.

Light the candle on the worship center, and call attention to the items there. Affirm that each item serves to record and pass on stories about who we are and where we have come from. Read the quote by Wendell Berry at the beginning of chapter 2 (page 27). Ask participants: **Who serves as the "rememberer" in your family; who serves as the rememberer(s) in this congregation?"** Say: Imagine a child in this congregation asking you what is the most important thing about being a Christian. What one thing would you want him or her to remember?

Offer these or similar words in prayer.

> **You are a storied God—and you would make of us a storied people, a people who remember, that we may be a people who hope. In Jesus Christ. Amen.**

ENCOUNTERING

Announce that Deuteronomy 26:1-12 will be offered as a litany to God, even as the text is structured around an offering brought to God. Explain that you will read one verse at a time. After each verse the group will respond by saying:

This is our story, and what we remember is what we hope.

Practice the group response several times so everyone is comfortable, then carry out the reading. Afterward, discuss:

- What in this story gives you hope; why?
- Why might this story be better affirmed by a group than an individual?
- Why does hope require remembrance?

REFLECTING

Ask participants to reflect on chapter 2 and the spiritual exercises (holding off, at this point, on the Day Four choices of action). Do so by asking individuals to share with the group what spoke most deeply to them in terms of affirmations, questions, disagreements, or new insights. If you have over twelve persons, form small groups to allow individuals more time to speak.

Discuss how these readings and exercises evoked stories and remembrances that form the faith and hope of participants. Ask how this congregation enables individuals and the community to remember what is needed—and to live accordingly.

SUPPORTING

Ask participants to identify the actions they chose in response to the Day Four spiritual exercise. Do this by inviting individuals to write those choices on newsprint or, with a smaller group, going around the circle and doing so.

Discuss how and where folks might work together, either as the whole group or in small groups, to support one another and perhaps combine efforts on one or more of the actions identified. If possible, use part of this time to plan or even do some of this common work.

CLOSING

Gather the group at the worship center. Invite participants to say aloud what they most need to remember from this session and a word or two about why. Emphasize that the story of faith needs those whose remembrance of God's saving activity empowers faithful stewardship and enduring hope.

Close by offering the final lines of chapter 2 (page 37) as a responsive commissioning. However, change "your" to "our" in the middle three lines, and change the final line to "You and I, and every beloved child of God." You begin with the first line ("Remember these things"). The group responds with the second line ("They tell our story"). Repeat that pattern for the third and fourth lines. Offer the final line in unison ("You and I, and every beloved child of God").

3 Hope: Trusting God's Leading

PREPARING

Materials: Advertisements that confuse "needs" and "wants," pictures that invite feelings of trust and security (a child in a parent's or grandparent's care; an elder who is at peace), if available, a picture of a shepherd); place these on or around the worship center.

Personal: This session underscores hope's reliance on trust and God's providing what we truly need (not necessarily what we simply want) in life. What causes you to trust another and/or trust in God? How do you differentiate between what you want in life and what you need and the role faith plays in discerning those differences?

GATHERING

Welcome participants and introduce any newcomers or visitors. Continue to use name tags as needed.

Light the candle on the worship center. Read aloud several of the advertisements. Invite participants to respond briefly to this question: **Are these talking about wants or needs? Why?** Look at the other pictures. Ask: **How might these images speak to the ads? Where and how is trust evoked in these pictures versus the first ones?**

Offer these or similar words in prayer.

> **We come to you in trust, O God. For we have known you as the One who provides for the deepest of our needs with your presence on the way. Amen.**

ENCOUNTERING

In earlier times, congregations sometimes sang hymns one line at a time as a leader "lined" it out. Explain this as the way that Psalm 23 will be read. You will read a verse (or portion thereof), and the group will respond by repeating the portion you spoke. Feel free to make the breaks in places other than verse endings. Lead the reading.

Ask individuals to read Psalm 23 from several different translations or paraphrases from the Bibles you have available, at least one of which should be a modern version (THE MESSAGE, for example).

Afterward discuss:

- How did these other readings of the psalm help you hear it differently?

- What might be a contemporary parallel to "shepherd" as an image of trust, provision, and encouraging presence?

REFLECTING

Ask participants to reflect on chapter 3 and the spiritual exercises (holding off, at this point, on the Day Four choices of action). Do so by asking individuals to share with the group what spoke most deeply to them in terms of affirmations, questions, disagreements, or new insights. If you have over twelve persons, form small groups to allow individuals more time to speak.

Discuss ways in which these readings and exercises addressed the ease or difficulty of trusting God's lead and/or the hope such leading provides. Consider how your congregation "shepherds" individuals and groups toward greater hope and trust.

SUPPORTING

Ask participants to identify the actions they chose in response to the Day Four spiritual exercise. Do this by inviting individuals to write those choices on newsprint or, with a smaller group, going around the circle and doing so.

Discuss how and where folks might work together, either as the whole group or in small groups, to support one another and perhaps combine efforts on one or more of the actions identified. If possible, use part of this time to plan or even do some of this common work.

CLOSING

Gather the group at the worship center and look again at the images there. Based on the conversations and activities, ask: **What images or ideas might you add that reveal trust in God's leading and provision and the hope that grows out of God's presence.** You might refer to the contemporary parallels to "shepherd" identified in the discussion at the end of ENCOUNTERING.

Close by using the "pilgrim prayer" rendering of Psalm 23 (page 49) at the end of chapter 3.

Divide its "You Are the One. . ." stanzas among individuals and partners (and trios, if you have a large group), so that everyone has at least one stanza to read.

4 Hope: Restoring Justice

PREPARING

Materials: Pictures and headlines (five or six total would be ideal) that illustrate various needs for justice or fairness in the world; place these on or around the worship center. Copies of Isaiah 65:17-25 (NRSV) for each participant. Sticky notes and pens. Newsprint sheet with last four lines of chapter 4 (page 61) written in large print.

Personal: This session will delve into relationship between hope and the restoration of justice, justice as both equity of relationships among us and fairness in the way life unfolds. Call to mind an experience, your own or another's, that sorely calls into question the possibility of justice in this world. How do you see God involved in the question of justice there? In what ways does restoration of justice require human effort and in what ways does it rely on God's working? And how does hope factor into your understandings of those two?

GATHERING

Welcome participants and introduce any newcomers or visitors.

Light the candle on the worship center. Give out sticky notes and pens. Ask individual participants to identify one of the pictures or headlines to focus on. Say: **In that situation, what would justice result in or how might it come to pass?** Have individuals then write a few words or phrase in response on a sticky note and place the sticky note on the picture. Allow time for participants to read all the notes.

Offer these or similar words in prayer.

> **You are the God of justice and righteousness, yet much in this world is not right or just. Show us where hope lies, and show us how hopes lives in the restoration of justice. Amen.**

ENCOUNTERING

Pass out the copy of Isaiah 65:17-25. Explain that you will read it aloud with the group's help. The group's help will be: every time the following words or phrases appear in the text, the group is to say them in unison with you: *create, creating, no more, they shall,* and *they shall not.*

Read the scripture. Afterward, discuss:

- **What does the restoration of justice rely on and consist of in this scripture?**

Form groups of two or three. Discuss:

- **Which of these hopes of restoration speaks most directly to you; why?**

REFLECTING

Ask participants to reflect on chapter 4 and the spiritual exercises (holding off, at this point, on the Day Four choices of action). Do so by asking individuals to share with the group what spoke most deeply to them in terms of affirmations, questions, disagreements, or new insights. If you have over twelve persons, form small groups to allow individuals more time to speak.

Discuss how these readings and exercises connected issues of justice and fairness with human and divine responsibilities. Talk about how your congregation not only engages individuals and groups to work for justice, but also nurtures hope in God's restoring of justice.

SUPPORTING

Ask participants to identify the actions they chose in response to the Day Four spiritual exercise. Do this by inviting individuals to write those choices on newsprint or, with a smaller group, going around the circle and doing so.

Discuss how and where folks might work together, either as the whole group or in small groups, to support one another and perhaps combine efforts on one or more of the actions identified. If possible, use part of this time to plan or even do some of this common work.

CLOSING

Gather the group at the worship center. Invite participants to identify what this session has raised up for them in terms of hope for and working toward God's promised restoration of justice. Call attention to the pictures and headlines at the worship center. Announce the session will close with a prayer that blends these images, the notes, and the Isaiah text.

Explain the process: you will raise up each picture or headline one at a time. If there are sticky notes on it, invite the one(s) who placed it to read what was written on the note (and if there are no notes on a picture, hold it up anyway).

Invite the group then to respond in unison with the final four lines of chapter 4 (page 61), printed on the newsprint sheet.

Lead the prayer, using all of the pictures and headlines.

5   Hope: Orienting to God's Blessing

PREPARING

Materials: A compass and, if available, a topographical map (ideally of your area or one close by); place these on the worship center. Copies of Matthew 5:3-12 and Luke 6:20-21 (New Revised Standard Version, NRSV) for each participant.

Personal: This session tries to orient our lives to what (and whom) God does and does not bless. Consider the community in which you live. If you were a newcomer, what might help "orient" you or provide a sense of direction for walking there? Consider your faith journey. What (and who) have been the "landmarks" that have provided you with a sense of direction on the path of faith? What do you associate with what is blessed of God?

GATHERING

Welcome participants and introduce any newcomers or visitors.

Light the candle on the worship center, and call attention to the compass and topographic map (if available). Ask: **When and where would these items be most useful?**

Have participants call out brief responses. Invite the group to consider how those responses might connect to the "wheres" and "whens" of our spiritual journeys. Invite participants to reflect silently on this question: **What do we rely on in our faith for orientation, and why?**

Offer these or similar words in prayer.

> **Holy One, we would journey toward you. But sometimes the way is hard to see, and sometimes we do not know which way to turn. Orient us to you. Amen.**

ENCOUNTERING

Form two groups. Have one group read aloud in unison Matthew 5:3-12, Then have the second group read aloud in unison Luke 6:20-21, 24-26.

Afterward discuss:

- How do these two versions speak to and complement each other?
- What blessings do you find most comforting, most challenging, most puzzling?
- In what ways do these words orient you toward God?

REFLECTING

Ask participants to reflect on chapter 5 and the spiritual exercises (holding off, at this point, on the Day Four choices of action). Do so by asking individuals to share with the group what spoke most deeply to them in terms of affirmations, questions, disagreements, or new insights. If you have over twelve persons, form small groups to allow individuals more time to speak.

Discuss how these readings and exercises lead us toward orientation (and sometimes disorientation) for the sake of discerning God's blessings. Consider the orientation your congregation's life and programs provide for individuals and groups who would journey toward faithfulness. What does your church use to orient its identity and mission?

SUPPORTING

Ask participants to identify the actions they chose in response to the Day Four spiritual exercise. Do this by inviting individuals to write those choices on newsprint or, with a smaller group, going around the circle and doing so.

Discuss how and where folks might work together, either as the whole group or in small groups, to support one another and perhaps combine efforts on one or more of the actions identified. If possible, use part of this time to plan or even do some of this common work.

CLOSING

Gather the group at the worship center. Say these or similar words:

We all need a sense of direction in life, a source of orientation that goes beyond personal intuition or "everybody else is doing it." We need insight into the ways and the ones God blesses, so that we can get our attitudes and actions on track. The Beatitudes provide one such source. They remind us and sometimes surprise us by their locating of God's blessings—and in so doing, they give us a sense of direction about the paths God invites us to follow and the ones God calls us to support. And blessed are the ones who find their lives so oriented.

Close by offering the final lines of chapter 5 (page 73, beginning with "This present moment and its possibilities. . ." as a benediction).

6   Hope: Finding Ourselves Loved

PREPARING

Materials: Pictures of families, at least one or two of which are torn (not cut) in half; place these on the worship center. Four copies of the Bible (NRSV).

Personal: This session invites us to find ourselves and others embraced by God's love, especially in the midst of division with others. Remember a time when you experienced God's love in a new way. How did that affect the way you felt about yourself? how you felt about others? Consider someone in your church with whom you disagree over a matter of theology. How does God's love for both of you shape how you relate to each other?

GATHERING

Welcome participants and introduce any guests or visitors.

Light the candle on the worship center, and pass around the pictures on the worship center. Invite silent reflection, then ask:

- Where do you see the signs of love?
- Where do you see the needs for love?
- Which of these pictures best portrays your current experience of family?
- Which of these pictures best portrays your current experience of church?

Offer these or similar words in prayer.

> Loving God, may we know and practice love. When we are at one and at peace, when we are torn and at odds, may we find and offer love's gift. Amen.

ENCOUNTERING

Ask volunteers to read the "voices" of the younger brother, the father, and the elder in the parable. You will narrate by reading the rest of

Luke 15:1-3, 11-32. Read the parable from the NRSV, providing copies to the readers as needed.

Afterward discuss:

- With whom do you empathize in this parable; why?
- What does hope consist of for each of the characters?
- What does love consist of for each of the characters?

REFLECTING

Ask participants to reflect on chapter 6 and the spiritual exercises (holding off, at this point, on the Day Four choices of action). Do so by asking individuals to share with the group what spoke most deeply to them in terms of affirmations, questions, disagreements, or new insights. If you have over twelve persons, form small groups to allow individuals more time to speak.

Discuss ways in which these readings and exercises address not only our coming to find ourselves loved but how that finding seeks to change us and our practice of love in the face of divisions. Hold this parable and these readings and exercises in tandem with a contemporary experience of division faced in or by your church. How might this parable's wisdom change the ways this conflict plays out?

SUPPORTING

Ask participants to identify the actions they chose in response to the Day Four spiritual exercise. Do this by inviting individuals to write those choices on newsprint or, with a smaller group, going around the circle and doing so.

Discuss how and where folks might work together, either as the whole group or in small groups, to support one another and perhaps combine efforts on one or more of the actions identified. If possible, use part of this time to plan or even do some of this common work.

CLOSING

Gather the group at the worship center. Invite reflection on what participants will take from this session about love in the midst of division and the hope that grows out of that for our lives and communities.

Form two groups and stand across from each other with the worship center in between. Place yourself between both groups and offer this line from the closing of chapter 6:

> **In Jesus Christ, we find ourselves and those from whom we are estranged, loved.**

Let the final lines of chapter 6 (page 85) serve as a responsive commissioning.

Group One: In that love we find our place.

Group Two: In that place we find our hope.

Group One: "You are always with me."

Group Two: "This brother of yours was dead and has come to life."

Group One: So Jesus told this parable to them. . . .

Group Two: So Jesus tells it to us.

All: That we who have been lost, divided, may be found.

Close by having participants greet those on the other side of the worship center.

7   Hope: Resurrecting Life

PREPARING

Materials: Symbols or pictures of death (photos of cemeteries and mourning, funeral or memorial service cards); place these on or around the worship center. Copies of 1 Corinthians 15:12-26, 55-58 (NRSV) for each participant.

Be sensitive to those who may have recently suffered the death of a friend or family member. Do *not* use pictures or symbols from those particular services.

Personal: This session explores what hope centered in resurrection does and does not affirm and its accompanying association with the "death of death." Recall a recent experience of grief or another reminder of your own mortality. What did that experience reveal to you about death, about hope? In what ways did resurrection influence your responses?

GATHERING

Welcome participants and introduce any newcomers or visitors.

Light the candle on the worship center. Ask participants to gather around the worship center. View the pictures, and touch the gathered symbols. Ask: **What thoughts, feelings, and experiences do these items evoke?** State that today's session has to do with hope grounded in resurrection. Even so, such hope always is set in the midst of death, for the power of such hope must inevitably confront the power of death with trust.

Offer these or similar words in prayer.

> **You walk with us, O God, in every place. You bid us to trust you. So when our journeys come to endings, may we trust you for beginnings. Amen.**

ENCOUNTERING

Distribute the printed copies of 1 Corinthians 15:12-26, 55-58. Explain that the group will read it responsively. Form two groups. One will read the even-numbered verses, the other the odd-numbered verses.

Afterward, discuss:

- **Does Paul's logic about the importance of resurrection to Christian faith convince you; why or why not?**
- **What hope does this passage speak to the pictures and symbols on the worship center; how?**

REFLECTING

Ask participants to reflect on chapter 7 and the spiritual exercises (holding off, at this point, on the Day Four choices of action). Do so by asking individuals to share with the group what spoke most deeply to them in terms of affirmations, questions, disagreements, or new insights. If you have over twelve persons, form small groups to allow individuals more time to speak.

Discuss how (or whether) these readings and exercises brought hope to bear on your experiences of death and wonderings about resurrection. Besides Easter services and ministry to families in times of grief, how does your church affirm resurrection not simply as a future hope but as the basis for life and witness today?

SUPPORTING

Ask participants to identify the actions they chose in response to the Day Four spiritual exercise. Do this by inviting individuals to write those choices on newsprint or, with a smaller group, going around the circle and doing so.

Discuss how and where folks might work together, either as the whole group or in small groups, to support one another and perhaps combine efforts on one or more of the actions identified. If possible, use part of this time to plan or even do some of this common work.

CLOSING

Gather the group at the worship center. Look again at the pictures and symbols of death. Invite participants to offer words or phrases raised in this session that would speak hope in the face of such realities and powers. Read aloud to the group the words of John Donne quoted in the beginning of the chapter.

As a closing commissioning, ask nine individuals to read one line each of the chapter's close, beginning with the line "What do we have to assure us. . ." (page 97). Clarify that the final line ("What say you?") will be spoken in unison by the whole group.

8   Hope: Confronting Separation

PREPARING

Materials: Cut a sheet of newsprint in half, or use a length from a roll of paper to create a banner. Write on it in large bold type: "If God is for us. . . . " Display the banner on or above the worship center.

Personal: This session aims to confront the very real experiences and powers that threaten or inflict separation with the word of God's favor and love from which we cannot be separated. Call to mind a powerful experience of separation in your life, whether the result of death or alienation in relationship or some other cause. What or who helped you through that experience; how? What does it mean for you to be assured God is "for you"?

GATHERING

Welcome participants and introduce any newcomers or guests.

Light the candle on the worship center. Read aloud the words on the banner (If God is for us. . . .). Invite participants to reflect on and call out, if they are comfortable doing so, a phrase that would complete that sentence with a positive statement (for example: I do not have to worry God is out to get me). Then invite participants to reflect on and call out, if comfortable doing so, a phrase that would complete that sentence with a question (for example: Why do innocent people suffer?). Affirm the truth of both the statements and the questions.

Offer these or similar words in prayer.

> **Your grace, O God, is your favor extended in our direction, on our behalf, for our sake. May we live with the courage such favor aims to inspire. Amen.**

ENCOUNTERING

Ask participants to close their eyes. Invite them to hear these words as if for the first time and to remember the most important thing they hear said. Read aloud Romans 8:31-39 slowly, pausing slightly where it seems a time for thought is needed. At the reading's end, ask participants to open their eyes. Invite them to identify aloud the most important thing they heard said and to state what made it important.

Afterward, discuss:

- What do Paul's words suggest about the community to whom he first wrote them?

- Who today might most need to hear Paul's words; why?

REFLECTING

Ask participants to reflect on chapter 8 and the spiritual exercises (holding off, at this point, on the Day Four choices of action). Do so by asking individuals to share with the group what spoke most deeply to them in terms of affirmations, questions, disagreements, or new insights. If you have over twelve persons, form small groups to allow individuals more time to speak.

Discuss ways in which these readings and exercises evoked remembrances of past or present separations. Where and in what did participants find hope through these readings and exercises? Consider how your church goes about not only supporting persons facing times of separation but embodying the message of God's favor in programs and ministries of compassion.

SUPPORTING

Ask participants to identify the actions they chose in response to the Day Four spiritual exercise. Do this by inviting individuals to write those choices on newsprint or, with a smaller group, going around the circle and doing so.

Discuss how and where folks might work together, either as a whole group or in small groups, to support one another and perhaps combine efforts on one or more of the actions identified. If possible, use part of this time to plan or even do some of this common work.

CLOSING

Gather the group at the worship center. Form a circle. Call attention to the banner: "If God is for us. . . ." Remind participants that Romans 8 confesses God's favor as the basis for hope from which we cannot be separated. Explain you will begin a blessing that personalizes this assertion. You will turn to the person on your left and say, "(name), God is for you." That person turns to his or her left, speaks the name of that individual, and repeats "God is for you." Continue around the circle until everyone has been so named and affirmed with the word of God's favor.

Close by inviting adults to offer the final lines of chapter 8 as a unison affirmation of faith. Begin with the line: "God is for us and has revealed that favor . . ." (page 109) and continue through the end.

9 Hope: Living Godward

PREPARING

Materials: Pictures or symbols that show newness or signs of re-creation (photos of a caterpillar and butterfly; photo of a newborn baby). If possible, include one or two items from your community (a photo of a building recently renovated; if your current church facility is not the original one, pictures of "before" and "after").

Personal: This session explores and affirms the promise of God's new creation through Revelation's vision of God's transforming presence among us.

GATHERING

Welcome participants. Express appreciation for their presence and participation throughout the weeks of this group experience.

Light the candle on the worship center. On a sheet of newsprint, write at the top: "God's new creation." Encourage participants to browse through photos and symbols on the worship center and to select one that illustrates in some way their hope for God's new creation. Ask participants to write a brief phrase on the newsprint sheet that expresses that hope (they need not identify the picture or symbol that generated it).

Offer these or similar words in prayer:

> You are the One who makes all things new—even us. Even when we are weary, even when the old weighs heavily on us. Come among us; fashion us and all things into your new creation. In Jesus Christ. Amen.

ENCOUNTERING

Read Revelation 21:1-5 aloud to the group. Ask two or three volunteers to read this same scripture from translations other than the New Revised Standard Version. Afterward, discuss:

- What differences do we hear in these various translations: in words, in images, in thoughts?
- What remains constant in these different versions in terms of the hope that is affirmed?
- If you could ask the author of Revelation one question or raise one issue you wish had been addressed here, what would it be?

REFLECTING

Ask participants to reflect on chapter 9 and the spiritual exercises (holding off, at this point, on the Day Four choices of action). Do so by asking individuals to share with the group what spoke most deeply to them in terms of affirmations, questions, disagreements, or new insights. If you have over twelve persons, form small groups to allow individuals more time to speak.

Discuss ways in which these readings and exercises addressed what it means to live Godward with hope. How are the promises of this text connected to what makes living with hope possible in our present world? Discuss how your congregation witnesses to and embodies the promise of God's new creation in its own life and programs.

SUPPORTING

Ask participants to identify the actions they chose in response to the Day Four spiritual exercise. Do this by inviting individuals to write those choices on newsprint or, with a smaller group, going around the circle and doing so.

Discuss how and where folks might work together, either as the whole group or in small groups, to support one another and perhaps combine efforts on one or more of the actions identified. If possible, use part of this time to plan or even do some of this common work.

CLOSING

Gather the group at the worship center. Look at the affirmations on the newsprint sheet created at the beginning of the session. Out of the conversations and activities of this session and from remembrances of past sessions, invite participants to add words or thoughts to the newsprint sheet that express the hope we are given. Add another newsprint sheet if needed. If possible, arrange for all the comments listed on the newsprint to be collated after the session, printed out, and given to the participants to keep with them both as reminder and encouragement.

Close by offering the final lines of chapter 9 as a litany affirmation of our faith and our calling to be a people of hope. You will begin by reading the first line ("Hope grounds us in a covenant struck by God's grace," pages 119–20), and the group will respond by reading the second line ("and we live Godward in our covenant relationships now"). Continue this pattern: you read the lines beginning with "hope"; the group responds with the lines beginning with "And we live Godward."

Personally greet and thank all participants for their involvement in this group before they leave.

Notes

Epigraph: Jürgen Moltmann, *The Coming of God: Christian Eschatology* (Minneapolis, MN: Fortress Press, 2004), 279.

CHAPTER 2

Epigraph: Wendell Berry, *That Distant Land: The Collected Stories* (Emery-ville, CA: Shoemaker & Hoard, 2004), 368.

CHAPTER 3

1. J. R. R. Tolkien, *The Fellowship of the Ring* (New York: Ballantine Books, 1965), 82.

CHAPTER 4

Epigraph: Jürgen Moltmann, *The Coming of God*, 118.

1. Walter Brueggemann, *Isaiah 40–66* (Louisville, KY: Westminster John Knox Press, 1998), 250.

CHAPTER 6

1. Annie Dillard, *An American Childhood* (Boston, MA: G. K. Hall & Co., 1987), 204.

CHAPTER 7

Epigraph: Jürgen Moltmann, *The Coming of God*, 65.

1. John Donne, "Sonnet X," from *English Literature: A College Anthol-ogy*, eds. Donald B. Clark, Leon T. Dickinson, Charles M. Hud-son, George B. Pace (New York: The MacMillan Co., 1960), 205–206.

CHAPTER 8

1. Jonathan Edwards, "Sinners in the Hands of an Angry God," from *Twenty Centuries of Great Preaching*, vol. III (Waco, TX: Word Books, 1971), 63.

About the Author

JOHN INDERMARK lives in southwest Washington state with his wife, Judy, an E-911 dispatcher and trainer. Their son, Jeff, works in the juvenile rehabilitation field for the state of Washington. John grew up in St. Louis, graduating from Northwest High School, St. Louis University, and Eden Theological Seminary. Ordained in the United Church of Christ, John served as a parish pastor for sixteen years. His ministry now is writing.

Hope: Our Longing for Home is John's seventh book published by Upper Room Books. John also writes materials for Christian education curricula. Current projects include *Seasons of the Spirit* and *The Present Word*. He wrote the New Testament materials for youth and leaders in *Crossings: God's Journey with Us*, a confirmation resource published in 2006 by Logos Productions, Inc.

In their spare time, John and Judy enjoy walking their region's trails and logging roads, beachcombing, puttering in the garden, and exploring Victoria and Vancouver Island in British Columbia. They also harbor dreams that the Seattle Mariners will win the World Series in their lifetime.